MW00849173

The Cuban Missile Crisis and the Cold War

A Short History with Documents

21 20 19 18   1 2 3 4 5 6 7

For further information, please address
        Hackett Publishing Company, Inc.
        P.O. Box 44937
        Indianapolis, Indiana 46244-0937

        www.hackettpublishing.com

Cover design by Rick Todhunter
Interior design by Laura Clark
Composition by Aptara, Inc.

Library of Congress Cataloging-in-Publication Data
Names: Getchell, Michelle, author.
Title: The Cuban Missile Crisis and the Cold War : A Short History with
  Documents / Michelle Getchell.
Description: Indianapolis : Hackett Publishing Company, 2018. | Series:
  Passages: Key Moments in History | Includes bibliographical references.
Identifiers: LCCN 2018010516 | ISBN 9781624667411 (pbk.) | ISBN
  9781624667428 (cloth)
Subjects: LCSH: Cuban Missile Crisis, 1962—Sources. | United
  States—Foreign relations—Soviet Union—Sources. | Soviet
  Union—Foreign relations—United States—Sources. | Cold War—
  History—Sources. | World politics—1945–1989—Sources. | Kennedy,
  John F. (John Fitzgerald), 1917–1963. | Khrushchev, Nikita Sergeevich,
  1894–1971.
Classification: LCC E841 .G48 2018 | DDC 972.9106/4—dc23
LC record available at https://lccn.loc.gov/2018010516

CONTENTS

LIST OF ILLUSTRATIONS

INTRODUCTION:
THE MAKING OF A GLOBAL CRISIS

On the morning of October 16, 1962, National Security Adviser McGeorge Bundy met with President John F. Kennedy to share some disturbing news. The previous day, the Central Intelligence Agency (CIA)—the premier foreign intelligence service of the United States—had discovered evidence of construction sites on Cuban soil for the emplacement of medium-range ballistic missiles. During an overflight of Cuba, the pilot of a U-2 (an ultra-high altitude reconnaissance aircraft designed for intelligence gathering) had taken photographs of one of the construction sites in San Cristóbal on the western side of the island. If the CIA's interpretation of the photographs was correct, it meant that nuclear weapons within range of targets in the mainland United States would soon be in the hands of avowed U.S. enemy Fidel Castro.

Castro had come to power on January 1, 1959, after waging a three-year guerrilla war against Cuban president Fulgencio Batista. While economic growth and standard of living had improved substantially under Batista, political freedoms were circumscribed and opponents of the regime were often imprisoned or worse.[1] Though Castro was not initially a Marxist, his hostility to the United States, much of which was a response to a long history of U.S. political and military interventionism in Latin America, encouraged him to turn to the Soviet Union for support. Two of Castro's closest advisers, his brother Raúl, and Argentine doctor and revolutionary Ernesto "Che" Guevara, both considered themselves Marxist-Leninists. They were sympathetic to Soviet communism and implacably opposed to what they viewed as U.S. imperialism in Latin America.

Castro and his comrades in arms were unhappy not only with U.S. interventionism in Latin America and the Caribbean generally, but also with the history of the U.S.-Cuban relationship specifically. In 1898, the United States went to war with Spain for the declared purpose of

---

1. On economic growth under Batista, see Jorge I. Domínguez, *Cuba: Order and Revolution* (Cambridge, MA: Harvard University Press, 1978), p. 72.

restoring peace to Cuba, where an anticolonial insurgency was threatening one of the few remaining vestiges of the decaying Spanish empire. The Spanish-American War, or War of 1898,[2] was a relatively brief conflict in which the United States won a decisive victory after sinking the remnants of the Spanish naval fleet off the shores of Cuba and the Philippines. Although anti-imperialist sentiment ran high in the United States at the time, President William McKinley believed the Cubans and Filipinos incapable of self-government; consequently, he saw no viable alternative to imposing a measure of U.S. control over the former Spanish colonial territories.

Fidel Castro and other Cuban revolutionaries were dissatisfied not only with the quasi-colonial historical relationship between Cuba and the United States, but were also resentful of U.S. support for Batista. Batista had legitimately governed Cuba from 1940 to 1944 but had then seized power in a coup in March 1952 and established a form of dictatorial rule. Judging his regime illegitimate and corrupt, Castro and other like-minded compatriots attacked the Moncada Army Barracks—the second largest military garrison in Cuba—on July 26, 1953. Many scholars view this date as the beginning of the Cuban Revolution.[3] Though the band of rebels was soundly defeated and Castro put behind bars, in May 1955 he was released under a general amnesty. Claiming to follow in the footsteps of famed revolutionary José Martí, who had led the late nineteenth-century Cuban insurrection against Spain, Castro then began organizing the 26th of July Movement (*Movimiento 26 de Julio*), named after the date of the failed Moncada Barracks attack. During a period of exile in Mexico, Castro linked up with other revolutionaries and returned to Cuba, where they launched an insurrection based in the mountains of the Sierra Maestra. Finally, on December 31, 1958, as Castro's 26th of July Movement forces marched into Havana, Batista fled the country.

---

2. Though traditionally referred to as the Spanish-American War, the conflict also involved Spain's rebellious colonies, Cuba and the Philippines. Thus, some scholars have recently sought to move away from a designation that excludes key actors. In the 1940s, the Cuban government officially renamed the conflict the Spanish-American-Cuban War to emphasize Cuban revolutionary nationalism as the cause of hostilities. For more on this, see Louis A. Pérez Jr., *The War of 1898: The United States and Cuba in History and Historiography* (Chapel Hill: University of North Carolina Press, 1998).

3. See, for instance, Antonio Rafael de la Cova, *The Moncada Attack: Birth of the Cuban Revolution* (Columbus: University of South Carolina Press, 2007).

alarming development. For them, the existence of NATO was incontrovertible evidence that the Western world was ganging up on them, for the express purpose of wiping the USSR off the map.

Two other momentous events of 1949 transformed the global strategic landscape. The Soviets successfully tested their own atomic bomb, several years before they could likely have developed the technology on their own. This was because Soviet spies had infiltrated the Manhattan Project and supplied Stalin's nuclear scientists with the technical details of American weapons systems. With each Cold War superpower in possession of nuclear bombs, the prospect of another global war became unthinkable. A nuclear first strike became perilous because of the enemy's ability to retaliate in kind. A nuclear confrontation would assuredly annihilate so much of humankind that the mere possession of these weapons would theoretically deter their use. But if nuclear weaponry could be used for deterrence purposes, it could also be used for coercive purposes. And the practice of nuclear deterrence could quickly bleed over into something much more dangerous—nuclear brinkmanship, a tactic of edging up to the brink of nuclear war in order to force the enemy into retreat. Nuclear brinkmanship was essentially the equivalent of a game of chicken, but with the survival of humankind at stake and the ability to escalate at a terrifying speed. This was an important lesson the Americans and Soviets would learn from the Cuban Missile Crisis.

The second transformational event of 1949 was the triumph of the Chinese Communist Party under Mao Zedong in China's civil war. Both developments produced profound anxiety in Washington. The communists under Mao had battled with Chiang Kai-shek's Nationalist Forces, supported by the United States, for years, but in 1949 Chiang was finally routed, and he and the remnants of his army fled to Taiwan. The communists established control over mainland China and allied with the Soviet Union. The Sino-Soviet Treaty of Friendship, Alliance, and Mutual Assistance, signed in February 1950, included provisions for the extension of Soviet economic aid to the newly established People's Republic of China (PRC) and the restoration of Soviet privileges in Manchuria.[23]

---

23. "Sino-Soviet Agreement Protocol," February 1950, History and Public Policy Program Digital Archive, Archive of Foreign Policy of the Russian Federation (AVPRF); obtained by Paul Wingrove, http://digitalarchive.wilsoncenter.org/document/111351, accessed June 20, 2017. For more on the Sino-Soviet alliance, see Austin Jersild, *The Sino-Soviet Alliance: An International History* (Chapel Hill: University of North Carolina Press, 2014).

Though this burgeoning friendship would founder on the shoals of ideological rivalry by the end of the decade, at the time of the communist victory in China, U.S. officials fretted over the fact that nearly half of the world's territory and population was now under communist control.

It would not be long before the fears of U.S. policymakers were realized. Just as Germany had been divided into Soviet and American occupation zones, so had Korea. The peninsula had been a Japanese colony since 1910, and when the Japanese surrendered in August 1945, the country was sliced in half at the 38th parallel—an arbitrary line on a map that ignored political and geographical realities.[24] Soviet troops flooded into the north, where a military government headed by communist Kim Il-Sung was installed, while in the southern American zone, ardent anticommunist nationalist Syngman Rhee came to power after U.N.-sponsored elections in 1948. Both leaders were determined to end the occupation and unite the Korean peninsula under their own control. In June 1950, having secured Stalin's approval, Kim and his troops crossed the 38th parallel and commenced hostilities. It was the first open invasion of internationally recognized borders since the end of the Second World War. Because the United Nations had been created explicitly for the purpose of collective security and to repel aggression of exactly this sort, and because President Truman himself was so committed to the success of the international organization, Kim's invasion demanded a determined response. The United Nations sent a peacekeeping force, composed largely of U.S. and South Korean troops. Chinese troops also entered the fray, on behalf of the North Koreans. The conflict revealed the new contours of warfighting in the nuclear age. Though both superpowers possessed atomic bombs, neither side detonated them. The Soviet nuclear arsenal was at this time unimpressive, and it is not clear that the Soviets could have effectively employed nuclear weaponry. The United States enjoyed a clear advantage in this realm, yet the Truman administration rejected the use of atomic weapons. Korea was not exactly a target-rich environment; thus, U.S. leaders sought to avoid escalating the war into a direct confrontation with the Soviets. The allied European powers balked at Truman's November 1950 statement that their use was "under consideration"—a statement most likely calculated to

24. William Stueck, *Rethinking the Korean War: A New Diplomatic and Strategic History* (Princeton, NJ: Princeton University Press, 2002), p. 12.

pressure the communist belligerents into seeking an end to the conflict.[25] But perhaps the most influential factor in Truman's calculus was a moral abhorrence of the sheer devastation wreaked by nuclear weapons. The effect of nuclear weapons was thus to keep the conflict relatively limited. After nearly three years of intermittent fighting and negotiating, a peace accord was finally reached. The armistice that ended the war left the status quo in place and Korea remained divided into a communist north and an anticommunist south.

Among other lasting consequences of the Korean War was the domestic implementation of NSC-68, a policy document drawn up by Paul Nitze, head of the State Department's Policy Planning Staff. The plan called for a massive military buildup in order to create a powerful deterrent against Soviet aggression. Nitze argued that U.S. policy must remain firm and vigilant so as to provide a powerful and credible check on the type of risk-taking and bold maneuvering that he believed would be an inevitable result of growing Soviet atomic capabilities. Any equivocation or vacillation, Nitze suggested, would be interpreted as a sign of weakness on the part of U.S. leaders and would be exploited as an opportunity to further erode American power and influence.[26] As we will see, this was a prescient prediction of what would happen in the Cuban Missile Crisis.

A New Front in the Cold War

With the situations in Europe and Asia seemingly stalemated, the former colonial possessions of the European powers became a Cold War battleground. These decolonizing and developing nations, located in Asia, Africa, and the Middle East, were known collectively as the "Third World." Alfred Sauvy, a French social scientist, coined the term to designate countries that refused to align with either Cold War superpower, but the phrase was imprecise at best. Although most Latin American countries had secured independence from Spain well over a century before the onset of the Cold War, many of them continued to face the same challenges of social, political, and economic development as other decolonizing

---

25. Gaddis, *We Now Know*, pp. 106–107.

26. Melvyn P. Leffler, *A Preponderance of Power: National Security, the Truman Administration, and the Cold War* (Stanford, CA: Stanford University Press, 1992), pp. 356–358.

states. This was at least in part due to the ongoing quasi-colonial relationship with the United States. While some Latin American leaders, like Argentina's Juan Perón, identified more with the Western "First World," others, like Fidel Castro, identified with the "Third World." The Cold War had a profound impact on the nations of the Third World, as their political elites sought to maneuver within an international system structured by the U.S.-Soviet competition.[27]

Stalin had effectively brought the Cold War to the Middle East as early as 1946, when he supported a separatist movement in Iran and pressured Turkey for territorial concessions and naval basing rights. Russian imperialists had for decades sought greater control over the Dardanelles, which locked in Russia's Black Sea fleet. The effect of Stalin's demands, however, was to reduce, not augment, Soviet influence in the region, as the Iranians and Turks looked to the West for security guarantees against Soviet penetration. Moreover, the purpose of Stalin's demands was to secure a compliant sphere of influence along Soviet borders. He had no particular interest in the decolonizing world as such, and was much more interested in Europe and Asia. China was in many ways undergoing its own process of decolonization, which involved recovering political control over territories that had been claimed by the European imperial powers. Though Stalin had provided support to both sides in the Chinese civil war—the Nationalists under Chiang Kai-shek and the Chinese Communist Party headed by Mao Zedong—this was out of concern for Soviet strategic interests in the Far East and not for the explicit purpose of securing the loyalties of the decolonizing world. Only after Stalin's death in 1953 and the rise to power of Nikita Khrushchev did the Soviet leadership begin to wage the Cold War in the Third World in earnest. This was not only due to the fact that his reign as Soviet premier coincided with the period of rapid postwar decolonization, but also because Khrushchev himself was a bold risk-taker who globalized the Kremlin's strategic vision and held a deeply romanticized view of national liberation movements.

In 1955, twenty-nine representatives from newly independent states in Africa and Asia convened in Bandung, Indonesia, for the first Afro-Asian Conference to discuss issues of peace, security, and development in a mutually cooperative environment free from the influence of the Cold War superpowers. The dominant impulse of the emerging neutralist bloc,

---

27. Odd Arne Westad, *The Global Cold War: Third World Interventions and the Making of Our Times* (New York: Cambridge University Press, 2005), p. 3.

which became formalized in 1961 as the Non-Aligned Movement, was to withdraw from the Cold War, aligning with neither the United States nor the Soviet Union. Nationalist leaders at the conference celebrated the formal demise of colonialism, with Indonesian president Sukarno proclaiming that "irresistible forces have swept the two continents" of Asia and Africa.[28] But while this was cause for celebration, it was not cause for complacency. It was imperative that the newly sovereign nations continue to struggle against continued threats from the imperial powers. Many of the delegates denounced the novel tactics of Western imperialism, which included the creation of regional pacts like the Southeast Asian Treaty Organization (SEATO). Though these regional defense alliances were promoted as a means of defending against the military threats purportedly posed by the Soviet bloc, many neutralist leaders viewed them as a way for the former imperial powers to continue exercising their influence under a new guise.[29] Among the most pressing items on the agenda of the Bandung Conference was the prospect of nuclear war. The delegates discussed the urgency of disarmament, and petitioned the United Nations to create an agency for the purpose of arms control. Though U.S. president Eisenhower had proposed an international organization for the regulation and promotion of peaceful uses of atomic power as early as 1953, it was not until 1957 that the United Nations created the International Atomic Energy Agency. Although many within what became the Non-Aligned Movement advocated strenuously for an immediate end to the arms race, others, including India, Pakistan, and China, developed their own nuclear weapons technology. The movement's unity and effectiveness would suffer from internal divisions such as the one over nuclear weapons. Moreover, Fidel Castro's Cuba would become a divisive influence in the movement, as Cuban leaders used it as a forum for condemning U.S. imperialism while promoting goodwill toward the Soviet Union.

While correctly identifying the significance of non-alignment, the Soviets and Americans approached the emerging Third World differently. The Soviets sought to encourage neutralist tendencies in the short term, believing that over the longer term these countries would ally themselves with the Soviet bloc. U.S. officials, on the other hand, viewed these neutralist tendencies as corrosive of Western power and influence, and sought to discourage them.

---

28. Sukarno, quoted in Vijay Prashad, *The Darker Nations: A People's History of the Third World* (New York: The New Press, 2007), p. 33.

29. Ibid., pp. 39–40.

Though U.S. policymakers were conditioned by their nation's history and its origins as an anticolonial rebellion against the British, and were thus sympathetic to the anticolonial sentiments of the non-aligned countries, they also feared that communist totalitarian regimes would arise to fill the vacuums of power left by the evacuation of colonial administrations.[30]

Lenin had written extensively about the importance of European colonial territories, and although Stalin himself was much more strategically focused on Europe and Asia, his successor Nikita Khrushchev quickly grasped the significance of the Third World and viewed it as a Cold War battleground. Khrushchev sent congratulatory messages to the participants of the Bandung Conference and sought to draw many of them into a closer relationship with the Soviet Union. After Castro came to power in Cuba, and Khrushchev embraced the revolutionary leader, they worked together to align the Non-Aligned Movement with Moscow, which tended to alienate more moderate members of the movement who saw these efforts as contrary to the very concept of non-alignment.

Khrushchev challenged Stalin's legacy in other ways as well. At the 20th Party Congress of the Soviet Communist Party in 1956, he delivered a speech condemning the terror and repression of the Stalin era (though he had personally drawn up lists of suspected "traitors" of the revolution as head of the Communist Party organization in Ukraine during the Great Terror) and repudiating the concept of inevitable hostility between the capitalist and socialist camps.[31] Khrushchev instead promoted the ideal of "peaceful coexistence," under which the United States and its allies (the so-called First World) and the Soviet Union and its allies (the so-called Second World) could compete in the economic, cultural, and ideological realms while avoiding an armed confrontation. The concept of peaceful coexistence was connected to decolonization, which Khrushchev lauded as a development of "world historical significance."[32]

---

30. See Jason Parker, "Cold War II: The Eisenhower Administration, the Bandung Conference, and the Reperiodization of the Postwar Era," *Diplomatic History*, Vol. 30, No. 5 (November 2006), pp. 867–892.

31. For more on Khrushchev's years in the Ukraine party, see Iurii Shapoval, "The Ukrainian Years, 1894–1949," in William Taubman, Sergei Khrushchev, and Abbott Gleason, eds., *Nikita Khrushchev* (New Haven, CT: Yale University Press, 2000), pp. 8–43.

32. Quoted in Mark Philip Bradley, "Decolonization, the Global South, and the Cold War, 1919–1962," in Leffler and Westad, eds., *Cambridge History of the Cold War, Volume I: Origins*, p. 475.

Somoza and Trujillo, who were perceived as bulwarks against communist influence in the hemisphere.

One of the policy tools that the United States employed was its dominant role in the inter-American system. The postwar creation of regional security pacts and organizations established a legal framework for U.S. leadership in the global anticommunist crusade. The Organization of American States (OAS) was designed alongside the United Nations, as the most recent iteration of an inter-American system that dated back to the late nineteenth century.[48] It was intended to facilitate cooperation among the states of the Western Hemisphere in the struggle against communism. In the concurrent creation of the United Nations and the Organization of American States, and during the process of drafting each organization's charter, a thorny issue arose: how to reconcile the authority and sovereignty of regional security organs with the universal scope and authority of the United Nations.

Many Latin American leaders—accustomed to solving regional problems on either a bilateral basis or under the auspices of a hemispheric organization—were concerned that the United Nations would provide the Soviet Union with a convenient cover for interference in the affairs of the Western Hemisphere.[49] At the behest of Latin Americans anxious to preserve regional autonomy, the U.N. charter included a chapter devoted to relations between the universal organization and other regional security organs. According to Articles 52 and 53, the U.N. charter did not preclude the existence of regional security arrangements and the Security Council would utilize such arrangements when appropriate, but regional organizations could embark upon no "enforcement action" without prior Security Council authorization.[50] The vague wording of the articles created a legal gray area that was interpreted differently by different actors. In practice, U.S. officials would argue that the Organization of American States should be the venue of first resort for the resolution of regional security issues. This was largely because the United States exercised a

---

48. See Renata Keller, "Building 'Nuestra America': National Sovereignty and Regional Integration in the Americas," *Contexto Internacional*, Vol. 35, No. 2 (July–December 2013), pp. 537–564.

49. Stephen C. Schlesinger, *Act of Creation: The Founding of the United Nations* (Boulder, CO: Westview Press, 2003), pp. 65–66.

50. Charter of the United Nations, Chapter VIII: Regional Arrangements, https://treaties.un.org/doc/Publication/CTC/uncharter.pdf, accessed June 6, 2017.

hegemonic influence in the OAS that could not be effectively replicated in the United Nations. The Soviets and their allies in the Western Hemisphere argued for a larger and more significant role for the United Nations in resolving Latin American crises. They believed that they could provide an effective counterweight to U.S. dominance of the OAS.[51]

Anticommunist officials in the United States and Latin America sought to build an Organization of American States strong enough to constitute a fortress against Soviet penetration of the Western Hemisphere. In 1947, the Inter-American Conference on the Maintenance of Continental Peace and Security convened in Rio de Janeiro. The United States and all twenty Latin American countries represented at the conference signed the Inter-American Treaty of Reciprocal Assistance, also known as the Rio Treaty. The treaty established a mechanism for collective security and codified the principles governing the inter-American system: the peaceful settlement of regional disputes, respect for the territorial integrity and political sovereignty of nations, and finally, a prohibition on intervention in the domestic affairs of member states. These principles provided a framework for the charter of the Organization of American States, which was created the following year in Bogotá.[52]

The foreign ministers gathered in Bogotá, Colombia, in 1948 for the Ninth Inter-American Conference of American States to draft a charter for the new organization. The charter upheld the principles of the Rio Treaty and also included chapters on economic, social, and cultural cooperation. The charter explicitly recognized the juridical equality of states, granting a vote to each member country and, unlike in the U.N. Security Council, the United States would not be allowed to exercise a veto. The U.S. delegation to the Bogotá conference was determined to discuss the dangers of international communism and devise approaches to combat it. Although some participants were initially reluctant to condemn the socialist bloc, rioting erupted in the capital on April 9, and rumors that the riots were instigated by communists ultimately weakened the opposition, leading to the unanimous approval of a hemisphere-wide anticommunist resolution. The resolution asserted the "interventionist

---

51. On the conflict between universalism and regionalism in the drafting of the U.N. charter, see Ruth B. Russell, *A History of the United Nations Charter: The Role of the United States, 1940–1945* (Washington, DC: Brookings Institution, 1958), pp. 688–712.

52. Carolyn M. Shaw, *Cooperation, Conflict, and Consensus in the Organization of American States* (New York: Palgrave Macmillan, 2004), pp. 53–55.

tendency" of "international communism," which was "incompatible with the concept of American freedom."[53] A paper prepared by the Policy Planning Staff of the U.S. Department of State in preparation for the Bogotá conference warned that although Soviet communism was only a "potential" as opposed to an "immediately serious" threat, bilateral or multilateral anticommunist agreements could be directed by regional dictators "against all political opposition, Communist or otherwise," a development that would surely drive the noncommunist left into the arms of the communists.[54]

One of the tensions at the heart of the inter-American system was between the U.S. preoccupation with hemispheric security and the Latin American emphasis on sovereignty, economic development, and nonintervention. In the run-up to the Bogotá conference, U.S. officials acknowledged that "to the Latin American countries economic development is a foremost objective of national policy," and cautioned that these countries were "increasingly dissatisfied over their economic relations with the U.S."[55] The Final Act of Bogotá, "The Preservation and Defense of Democracy in America," sought to guard against the influence of "international communism" or "any totalitarian doctrine," and recognized that in order to do so, it was essential to adopt an economic policy aimed at raising the living standards of the peoples of Latin America.[56] At the same time, U.S. officials seemed to understand that their support for right-wing dictators in the hemisphere would undermine democratic development, as these regional strongmen employed tactics "very similar to Communism as concerns totalitarian police state methods."[57] U.S. foreign policymakers thus exercised a double standard when it came to

---

53. Quoted in J. Lloyd Mecham, *The United States and Inter-American Security, 1889–1960* (Austin: University of Texas Press, 1961), p. 429.

54. "Paper Prepared by the Policy Planning Staff," March 22, 1948, *Foreign Relations of the United States* [hereafter, *FRUS*], 1948, Volume IX: The Western Hemisphere (Washington, DC: U.S. Government Printing Office, 1972), pp. 198–199.

55. "A Positive Program of United States Assistance for Latin America," *FRUS*, 1948, Volume IX: The Western Hemisphere (Washington, DC: U.S. Government Printing Office, 1972), p. 5.

56. "Final Act of Bogotá," in ibid., pp. 193–194.

57. "Paper Prepared by the Policy Planning Staff," March 22, 1948, *FRUS*, 1948, Volume IX: The Western Hemisphere (Washington, DC: U.S. Government Printing Office, 1972), p. 197.

democracy in Latin America, tolerating authoritarian regimes as long as they were anticommunist.

Nowhere was the tension between the competing interests of the United States and Latin America more apparent than at the Tenth Inter-American Conference in Caracas, Venezuela, in March 1954. Some contemporary observers noted the irony of convening a conference to defend the hemisphere against totalitarianism in a country led by a dictator, Marcos Pérez Jiménez. Pérez Jiménez, who routinely imprisoned or executed his political opponents, enjoyed the firm backing of the United States. Not only did he keep the oil flowing to his northern neighbor, but he also adhered to a strict anticommunist line.

One of the main U.S. objectives for the conference was to establish that "the communist movement is international in scope and directed from Moscow," and "as such it constitutes intervention in the affairs of the Americas."[58] Because of the inter-American system's rejection of external intervention in the domestic affairs of member states, it was imperative to define communism as external intervention. If communism was viewed as a domestic political movement, there would be no legal basis for U.S. intervention. U.S. secretary of state John Foster Dulles conceded all of this in a cabinet meeting in late February, acknowledging that "the major interest of the Latin American countries at this conference would concern economics whereas the chief U.S. interest is to secure a strong anti-Communist resolution which would recognize Communism as an international conspiracy instead of regarding it merely as an indigenous movement."[59] If the United States could effectively define communism as external aggression, then U.S. intervention to combat the dangerous influence of this foreign ideology could be justified as an extension of the Monroe Doctrine.[60]

The U.S. delegation to Caracas, headed by Secretary Dulles, presented a draft resolution, titled "Intervention of International Communism in

---

58. "Memorandum by the Assistant Secretary of State for Inter-American Affairs (Cabot) to the Acting Secretary of State," February 10, 1954, in *FRUS*, 1952–1954, Volume IV: The American Republics (Washington, DC: U.S. Government Printing Office, 1983), p. 279.

59. "Minutes of a Cabinet Meeting, Held at the White House, 10:10 a.m., February 26, 1954," in ibid., pp. 300–301.

60. "Memorandum of Discussion at the 189th Meeting of the National Security Council on Thursday, March 18, 1954," in ibid., p. 304.

was reluctant to declare war on Spain, after a series of diplomatic failures and military fiascoes, the United States entered the war on Cuba's behalf. The fight did not last long. The last remnants of the Spanish empire slipped away after the U.S. Navy destroyed the Spanish fleet. Though U.S. forces had entered the fray with the declared purpose of helping Cuba achieve independence, the treaty that ended hostilities forced the island into a quasi-colonial relationship with the United States, whereby U.S. officials exercised control over Cuban foreign policy, secured basing rights at Guantánamo Bay, and reserved the authority to intervene in the domestic political affairs of the nation.[73] This relationship engendered resentment and hostility among the Cuban people and fertilized the soil in which Castro's opposition to U.S. foreign policy took root.

As a law student at the University of Havana, Castro traveled in radical student activist circles, even campaigning (unsuccessfully) for the presidency of the Federation of University Students. In 1947, he joined the Partido del Pueblo Cubano-Ortodoxo, or the Orthodox Party, a left-wing populist group that opposed the corruption and violence of the Ramón Grau San Martín regime. After participating in failed uprisings to overthrow dictators in the Dominican Republic and Colombia, Castro began plotting the ouster of Cuban president Fulgencio Batista, who had governed the country legitimately from 1940 to 1944. After attaining power in a military coup in 1952, Batista declared the Cuban Communist Party, the Partido Socialista Popular (Popular Socialist Party, PSP), illegal. The PSP was a Moscow-oriented party that took its marching orders from the Kremlin. After Batista's power play, the party went underground, where it continued organizing and propagandizing on behalf of the Soviet Union. With Nikita Khrushchev's emergence as Stalin's successor, "peaceful coexistence" became the order of the day. This did not mean that the Cold War was over—far from it. Rather, the Cold War would be waged via peaceful methods, through which the Soviets would eventually surpass the United States by all measures of technological, economic, social, and cultural progress. This was the line adopted by the PSP while Castro traveled the road from political exile to revolutionary hero.

On July 26, 1953, Castro spearheaded an attack on the Moncada Barracks, the largest military installation in Cuba. The attack quickly failed and the surviving conspirators were imprisoned and later released

---

73. For more, see Pérez Jr., *The War of 1898*.

into exile. Castro spent his exile in Mexico City, where he linked up with Ernesto "Che" Guevara, a peripatetic Argentine medic who had become politically radicalized by his travels through Latin America and his first-hand observation of the CIA-backed coup that overthrew Guatemala's second democratically elected president. Castro also came into contact with Alberto Bayo Giroud, a Cuban-born veteran of the Spanish Civil War and the insurgency against Nicaraguan dictator Anastasio Somoza García in the 1940s.[74] Bayo trained Castro and his recruits in the art of guerrilla warfare, and in 1956, the rebels set sail for Cuba aboard the *Granma*, a yacht that was so overloaded it almost sank in a storm.[75] Miraculously, they survived the voyage and landed on the shores of Oriente province, where Batista's men were waiting. Decimated by superior military force, Castro and his few fellow survivors retreated into the Sierra Maestra mountains to wage a guerrilla war, forming the 26th of July Movement, named after the date of the failed Moncada attack. After two years of guerrilla warfare had undermined Batista's authority, the United States officially suspended arms shipments to his regime. Batista had been violating the terms of the defense agreements with the United States, which prohibited him from using U.S.-supplied weaponry against his own people. The Cuban public viewed the suspension of U.S. arms shipments as a withdrawal of U.S. support for Batista, which further undermined the legitimacy of his government and the morale of his military.[76] After the 26th of July Movement gained the support of the peasantry and a large number of moderate political groups in the country, the struggle finally came to an end on New Year's Eve 1958, when Batista fled the country and Castro's forces marched triumphantly into Havana.

Policymakers in Washington and Moscow alike were unsure what to think. Although Castro was known as a political dissident and guerrilla fighter, his ideological convictions were obscure. Was he a nationalist who would fiercely protect the national interests and sovereignty of Cuba or was he a communist who would look to Moscow for ideological and strategic guidance? In Washington, the Eisenhower administration was deeply concerned about the potential convergence of radical nationalism

74. Thomas G. Paterson, *Contesting Castro: The United States and the Triumph of the Cuban Revolution* (New York: Oxford University Press, 1994), pp. 16–18.

75. Tad Szulc, *Fidel: A Critical Portrait* (New York: William Morrow, 1986), p. 43.

76. Domínguez, *Cuba: Order and Revolution*, p. 64.

U.S. and Regional Responses to the Cuban Revolution

The firm anticommunism of the United States and many other countries of the Western Hemisphere translated into policies designed to isolate Cuba, weaken its revolutionary leadership, and create the conditions necessary for the ultimate overthrow of Fidel Castro. Such policies were implemented at the national and regional levels, as the U.S. government adopted first economic, then political, and finally, military measures to support its policy objective of regime change in Cuba. Regional policy was orchestrated in the Organization of American States, and frequently followed the line set by the United States.

In fact, before the 26th of July Movement had triumphed over Batista, the Eisenhower administration had taken steps to prevent it from coming to power. Though well aware that Batista would have to go, officials in the U.S. Department of State sought to generate regional interest in a mediated settlement to the conflict, perhaps under the auspices of the Organization of American States. There were few takers. Most Latin American officials sympathized with the rebel movement, rejected the possibility of external intervention, or simply believed that the OAS was too ineffective to resolve the crisis.[114] After Castro came to power, Eisenhower and his successor, John F. Kennedy, continued to use the OAS to coordinate regional policy toward Cuba.

Though the Eisenhower administration had initially approached Castro with caution, a series of tit-for-tat reprisals soured U.S.-Cuban relations. In April 1959, just four months after seizing power, Castro announced that elections, part of the 26th of July Movement's platform since 1953, would not be held. Then, confusingly, though Castro had refused to discuss economic aid during his visit to the United States, at a meeting of the OAS economic council, he called for the United States to issue over the course of ten years a thirty billion dollar loan to Cuba for economic development. In May, an agrarian reform law confiscating large landed estates, which affected several U.S. firms, was implemented, and then in June, Castro replaced many of the moderates in his government with communists.[115] Castro moved to consolidate power in his

---

114. Paterson, *Contesting Castro*, p. 213.

115. Domínguez, *To Make a World Safe for Revolution*, pp. 18–19.

own hands, and appointed to leadership positions those whose loyalty to him personally was unquestioning. During the same period, he escalated his anti-U.S. rhetoric, and by the fall of 1959, relations with the United States had become tense, if not openly hostile.

One of the thorniest issues in U.S.-Cuban relations involved sugar. The Cuban economy had long depended on the profits from sugarcane cultivation and exports. The United States had been one of the largest consumers of Cuban sugar, and Castro early on demonstrated an ambiguous approach to the U.S. sugar quota, which provided special protections for Cuban sugar imports to the United States. In February, a mere month after attaining power, he announced that the sugar quota would be rescinded because it kept Cuba in a state of dependency on the United States. Rather than cutting the sugar quota, U.S. officials actually increased it. In the fall of 1959, the Eisenhower administration began to seriously consider reductions in the quota, and Castro responded with accusations of economic aggression against his regime.[116] In February, the Cubans and Soviets publicly signed their first official bilateral agreement, according to which the Soviets would purchase a million tons of sugar a year for five years, lend Cuba one hundred million dollars for economic development, and sell petroleum to Cuba for less than market price. Then, on March 4, 1960, *La Coubre*, a French ship carrying Belgian weapons and ammunition for the Cuban government exploded in Havana harbor, and Castro wasted no time blaming it on the United States. Though he admitted that "we do not have full proof" that the explosion was a result of U.S. sabotage, the incident further eroded relations.[117] Less than two weeks later, Eisenhower authorized the CIA to begin drawing up plans for a covert invasion of Cuba to oust Fidel Castro from power.

In June, relations with the United States deteriorated even further after the Texaco refinery in Cuba refused to process 20,000 barrels of Soviet crude oil. Texaco officials had consulted with the State Department before reaching this decision and had been informed that "if a decision not to process Russian crude was made this would be consonant with U.S. Government policy."[118] The Cuban Petroleum Institute

---

116. Ibid., pp. 24–25.

117. Quoted in ibid., p. 24.

118. Quoted in Morris H. Morley, *Imperial State and Revolution: The United States and Cuba, 1952–1986* (New York: Cambridge University Press, 1987), p. 104.

responded by seizing the refinery. Shell and Standard Oil also declined to refine the crude, and their facilities were confiscated in turn. On July 3, the U.S. Congress approved the Sugar Act, which granted the president discretionary authority to cut Cuba's sugar quota. Eisenhower did so on July 6—by a whopping 95 percent. The Soviets responded with an announcement that they were prepared to purchase all of the sugar that the United States refused.

As U.S.-Cuban relations broke down, Castro repeatedly warned his benefactors in the Kremlin of the threats that U.S. hostility posed to his revolution. Such warnings were likely calculated to convince the Soviet leadership to provide more military support to the Cuban Revolution. If that was indeed Castro's intention, it was successful. On July 9, 1960, at the All-Russian Teachers' Congress in Moscow, Khrushchev delivered a speech condemning U.S. imperial aggression against Cuba, and swore to "do everything to support Cuba and its courageous people in the struggle for the freedom and national independence they have won under the leadership of . . . Fidel Castro." He then referenced the way the Cuban Revolution had altered geostrategic realities, with a warning that "the United States is not as inaccessibly distant from the Soviet Union as it used to be." Khrushchev promised that Soviet artillerymen would "support the Cuban people with their rocket fire if the aggressive forces in the Pentagon dare to launch an intervention against Cuba."[119] For obvious reasons, the speech set off alarm bells in the Eisenhower administration. The U.S. president himself responded with a statement later that day, describing Khrushchev's statements as "the effort of an outside nation and of international communism to intervene in the affairs of the Western Hemisphere." Eisenhower pledged "in the most emphatic terms that the United States will not be deterred from its responsibility by the threats Mr. Khrushchev is making."[120] The U.S. ambassador in Havana reported back to the State Department about a rumor to the effect that Castro had been "caught entirely off base" by Khrushchev's statement. The ambassador had apparently heard from multiple sources that Castro was "perfectly furious about a development which puts Cuba entirely under

---

119. Editorial Note, *FRUS*, 1958–1960, Vol. VI: Cuba, Document 549, https://history
.state.gov/historicaldocuments/frus1958-60v06/d549, accessed June 29, 2017.

120. Ibid.

the Soviet wing."[121] As much as Castro desired Soviet military assistance, he was not prepared to sacrifice Cuban sovereignty or independence to secure it.

The U.S. secretary of state characterized Khrushchev's threats as the "most fundamental challenge" that the inter-American system had ever faced. Despite the obvious danger, he believed that some Latin American countries would resist taking collective action to dispel the threat. For domestic political reasons, many governments in the hemisphere could not act decisively against Castro, because of his popularity among the Latin American masses.[122] The principle of nonintervention was also of paramount importance to the countries of the hemisphere that conducted their foreign policies independently of U.S. goals and desires.[123] In order to counter this potential hemispheric opposition to interventionist measures against Castro, U.S. diplomats prepared a case against Cuba in the hopes of convincing the Latin American states to take action.

In August 1960, the Council of Foreign Ministers of the Organization of American States convened in San José, Costa Rica. The resulting Declaration of San José, clearly aimed at Cuba, "condemn[ed] energetically the intervention or the threat of intervention . . . by an extracontinental power in the affairs of the American republics," and "reject[ed] . . . the attempt of the Sino-Soviet powers to make use of the political, economic, or social situation of any American state, inasmuch as that attempt is capable of destroying hemispheric unity and endangering the peace and security of the hemisphere."[124] Though most of the Latin American members lined up behind the United States in issuing the declaration, the Mexican delegation to the conference opposed the condemnation of Cuba, and appended a statement to the declaration denying

---

121. "Letter from the Ambassador in Cuba (Bonsal) to the Assistant Secretary of State for Inter-American Affairs (Rubottom)," July 13, 1960, *FRUS*, Vol. VI: Cuba, Document 554, pp. 1008–1009.

122. For more on the nexus between domestic politics and foreign policy in the case of Mexico, see Renata Keller, *Mexico's Cold War: Cuba, the United States, and the Legacy of the Mexican Revolution* (New York: Cambridge University Press, 2015).

123. "Circular Telegram from the Department of State to Certain Diplomatic Missions in the American Republics," July 11, 1960, *FRUS*, Vol. VI: Cuba, Document 552, pp. 1006–1007.

124. Declaration of San José, Costa Rica, adopted at the Seventh Meeting of Consultation of Ministers of Foreign Affairs (Washington, DC: General Secretariat of the Organization of American States, 1960).

the Cubans with military materiel, and there was a rapid buildup in the capabilities of the Cuban armed forces from the fall of 1960 through the spring of 1961. The CIA estimated that the Revolutionary Army was 32,000 strong and that the militias were close to 200,000 in number, and that these forces had access to between thirty and forty thousand tons of Soviet bloc–supplied weaponry, valued at thirty million dollars.[141] Meanwhile, the CIA was ill equipped, as the Kennedy administration refused to allocate the most modern weapons for fear that they would be easily traced back to the United States. Thus, instead of deploying more efficient A-5 aircraft for the initial airstrikes, as requested, obsolete B-26 bombers were used, hampering the effectiveness of air support. Modern rifles and other auxiliary equipment were also refused.[142] The agency's maritime capabilities, moreover, were painfully inadequate, lacking trained personnel, equipment, boats, bases, and doctrine.[143] Furthermore, Castro's tightened security measures prevented the development of a strong Cuban-based intelligence network and reduced opportunities to strengthen anti-Castro guerrilla groups.[144] In sum, the changes in the planning for Operation Zapata and the flawed assumptions upon which they were based reduced the effectiveness of the operation without enhancing plausible deniability of the U.S. role.

In fact, the Cubans were well aware of the impending invasion. In November 1960, the Cubans sent reports to Moscow that an exile force was being trained in Guatemala. The U.S. news media also reported on the training activities of anti-Castro Cuban exiles. Though Castro had plenty of spies in the exile movement, open, public-source reports provided him with almost all of the information he needed to thwart the attack.[145] President Kennedy himself lamented that Castro "didn't need agents over here," because "all he had to do was read our papers."[146] In

---

141. Ibid., p. 52.

142. Ibid., pp. 55–56.

143. Ibid., p. 89.

144. "An Analysis of the Cuban Operation," by the Deputy Director (Plans), CIA, January 18, 1962, in ibid., p. 145.

145. On Castro's intelligence and espionage apparatus, see Brian Latell, *Castro's Secrets: Cuban Intelligence, the CIA, and the Assassination of John F. Kennedy* (New York: St. Martin's Press, 2012).

146. John F. Kennedy, quoted in Kornbluh, ed., *Bay of Pigs Declassified*, p. 2.

early April, the CIA intercepted a cable from the Soviet embassy in Mexico City warning that an attack was scheduled for April 17. The U.S. hand in the operation had already been tipped.

Nevertheless, on April 17, the amphibious landing operation was launched on schedule. It was riddled with errors at both the planning and operational levels. The brigade was detected before it even landed, and contrary to expectations that the landing site would be obscured and unpopulated, it was in fact bathed in bright light from a nearby lighthouse, and populated by local militia and a regular infantry battalion. Unsure whether this was only one of many landing sites, Castro withheld his tank battalions until certain that the main invasion force was at Playa Girón.[147] Among other mishaps, the invaders quickly ran out of ammunition, and the few airdrops of supplies that were made were scooped up by Castro's forces.[148] Only Cuban exiles crewed the aircraft that were used for drop and combat missions, and of the eleven Cuban-manned B-26s, only three returned to base. Four were shot down by Cuban antiaircraft weapons. The following day, the remaining invasion force requested more air support. Four American-crewed aircraft answered the request; two were shot down by Castro's T-33s. Two more American crews sortied; four fliers were either killed in action or shot down and summarily executed.[149] Even as Castro's infantry and air force summarily dispatched the invaders, Khrushchev sent Kennedy a note proclaiming that the Soviets would provide "all necessary assistance in beating back the armed attack on Cuba."[150] The few remaining survivors of Brigade 2506, lacking ammunition and air support, and facing a well-armed contingent of some 20,000 Cuban militiamen and regular troops, began surrendering on the afternoon of April 19.[151] Of the approximately 1,300 members

---

147. Trumbull Higgins, *The Perfect Failure: Kennedy, Eisenhower, and the CIA at the Bay of Pigs* (New York: W. W. Norton, 1987), pp. 138–139.

148. Ibid., p. 143

149. Kornbluh, ed., *Bay of Pigs Declassified*, p. 98.

150. Quoted in Higgins, *The Perfect Failure*, p. 145.

151. Ibid., p. 149. Thanks to back channel diplomacy between Castro and U.S. negotiator James Donovan, 1,113 prisoners of the Bay of Pigs operation were released in the spring of 1963. See William M. LeoGrande and Peter Kornbluh, *Back Channel to Cuba: The Hidden History of Negotiations between Washington and Havana* (Chapel Hill: University of North Carolina Press, 2015), p. 67.

regime.[169] The CIA, meanwhile, was busy preparing an invasion directed at the "physical destruction of the leaders of the revolution."[170] Although the message included no direct appeal for military aid, the meticulous detailing of the existential threats facing the Cuban Revolution suggests that such aid was exactly what the Cuban government was hoping for. Moreover, the letter revealed the extent to which Cuban leaders blamed the United States for the consequences of Cuba's own interventionist foreign policy in the Western Hemisphere. In response, Khrushchev proclaimed that "our hearts are with you, heroes of Cuba, in defense of your independence and freedom from American imperialism." At the 22nd Congress of the Soviet Communist Party, which convened a week after the receipt of the Cuban telegram, Anastas Mikoyan declared that Cuba had taken "the road of true liberation from the yoke of the monopolies . . . and is building a socialist life."[171] Despite these declarations of support, admiration, and ideological fraternity, the Soviets were still hesitant to make a formal military commitment to the Cuban Revolution.

Castro ratcheted up his rhetoric even further, following his declaration of Cuba as a socialist revolution with the claim in December 1961 that he personally was a Marxist-Leninist, and had been since his days as a student at the University of Havana. The Soviets were not sure how to respond to Castro's announcement. They understood the responsibility that a guarantee of military protection of the Cuban Revolution would entail and were circumspect in their response to Castro's bid. According to Kiva Maidanik, a scholar of Latin America in the Soviet Institute of World Economy and International Relations (IMEMO), though the Soviet leadership certainly reveled in the humiliation and loss of U.S. prestige that Castro's announcement entailed, Castro's claims to be not just a communist, but a leader of world communism, were highly troubling. "To us," Maidanik confided in an interview with scholars James G. Blight and Philip Brenner, "this is an impossible concept because *we* decide who is and is not a communist. And of course, there is no 'leader' other than ourselves." Maidanik claims that the Soviet leadership viewed Castro with suspicion from the moment of his announcement, fearing that the Cubans would reveal themselves as "heretics" who had succumbed to the

---

169. Ibid., Ll. 96–99.

170. Ibid., L. 100.

171. Quoted in Jacques Lévesque, *The USSR and the Cuban Revolution: Soviet Ideological and Strategic Perspectives, 1959–1977* (New York: Praeger, 1978), p. 35.

"Chinese virus."[172] The Chinese at the time were vying with the Soviets for leadership of the communist movement in the Third World, and the Soviets actively sought to reduce Chinese influence.[173] The Cubans had shown signs of moving toward the Chinese camp, and some Kremlin policymakers were unsure what to think. Many in the Soviet leadership, moreover, feared that Castro's statements would complicate his domestic political situation and openly invite U.S. hostility, heightening the prospect of U.S. military intervention and putting Khrushchev's pledges of protection to a very public test.[174]

Therefore, the Soviet press, rather than trumpeting the triumph of a Marxist-Leninist regime in the Western Hemisphere, remained uncharacteristically silent about this momentous development.[175] It is notable that until April 11, 1962, over four months after Castro declared that he was a Marxist-Leninist and had been since his student days, Soviet newspaper *Pravda* refrained from referring to Cuba as "socialist" or Castro as a "communist."[176] Khrushchev's decision to station missiles on Cuban territory was made shortly after the formal recognition of Cuba as a socialist state.[177]

The Soviets interpreted the failed outcome of the invasion as further evidence of the changing correlation of forces—the imperialist bloc was in decline and socialism was on the rise. "The failure of the attempt to export counter-revolution to Cuba," wrote one theorist, "shows that the possibilities of the revolutionary liberation movement are enormously greater than before."[178] At the same time, however, the timing of the invasion proved problematic for Khrushchev—he was forced to come to the defense of the Cuban Revolution right in the middle of preparations for the historic Vienna summit with President Kennedy, scheduled for

---

172. James G. Blight and Philip Brenner, *Sad and Luminous Days: Cuba's Struggle with the Superpowers after the Missile Crisis* (Lanham, MD: Rowman & Littlefield, 2002), p. 108.

173. For more on the Sino-Soviet split and the underdeveloped world, see Jeremy Friedman, *Shadow Cold War: The Sino-Soviet Competition for the Third World* (Chapel Hill: University of North Carolina Press, 2015).

174. Pavlov, *Soviet-Cuban Alliance*, p. 22.

175. Lévesque, *The USSR and the Cuban Revolution*, pp. 31–32.

176. Ibid.

177. Ibid., p. 38.

178. Quoted in ibid., p. 29.

June. A strong defense of Cuba increased U.S.-Soviet tensions during a period in which "peaceful coexistence" dominated the Soviet party line and Khrushchev was seeking to improve relations with the United States.

Moreover, the Bay of Pigs strengthened the position of hardliners in the Kremlin and solidified an impression of President Kennedy as indecisive.[179] That impression was reinforced at the June summit in Vienna, where Khrushchev had planned not necessarily to engage in concrete negotiations, but rather to merely take stock of the U.S. leader. In conversations between the two, Khrushchev informed Kennedy, "Castro is not a Communist but US policy can make him one."[180] According to at least one former Soviet official, after meeting and discussing international affairs with his U.S. counterpart, Khrushchev determined that Kennedy was a "mere 'boy' who would be vulnerable to pressure," and considered subjecting him to "a test of strength."[181] Indeed, at the end of the first day of the summit, Kennedy complained to his aides that Khrushchev had treated him "like a little boy," and admitted, "Because of the Bay of Pigs" Khrushchev "thinks . . . that I'm inexperienced."[182] This perception of Kennedy as weak and indecisive contributed to Khrushchev's decision to station nuclear missiles in Cuba. Khrushchev seems to have believed that the Kennedy administration would simply accept the altered strategic balance as a fait accompli.

The Bay of Pigs also provided the Soviets an opportunity to enhance their image in the Third World by linking the struggle of the Cuban people to the trials and tribulations of the decolonizing world. As soon as the fiasco hit the headlines and airwaves, the Soviet Afro-Asian Solidarity Committee adopted a resolution demanding of the imperialists, "Hands off Cuba!" Occurring on the Solidarity Committee's designated "African Freedom Day," the U.S. invasion was denounced as a "monstrous atrocity." "The time has passed," declared the committee, "when the imperialists could through force of arms subjugate an entire people

---

179. Arkady N. Shevchenko, *Breaking with Moscow: The Compelling Story of the Highest Ranking Soviet Defector* (London: Grafton Books, 1986), p. 182.

180. Memorandum of Conversation between President Kennedy and Premier Nikita Khrushchev at the Vienna Summit, June 3, 1961, *FRUS*, 1961–1963, Volume V: Soviet Union, Document 85, https://history.state.gov/historicaldocuments/frus1961-63v05 /d85, accessed June 6, 2017.

181. Shevchenko, *Breaking with Moscow*, p. 183.

182. Quoted in Rasenberger, *The Brilliant Disaster*, p. 347.

Figure 3. Soviet premier Nikita Khrushchev and U.S. president John F. Kennedy at the Vienna summit in June 1961. (U.S. Department of State/public domain)

to its will." Now, the colonialists were opposed by the "powerful socialist camp," as well as by the "many millions of peace-loving peoples in the countries of Asia, Africa, and Latin America, who have firmly committed to bringing a decisive and permanent end to colonialism." The committee concluded with the resounding cry, "Long live the unity and solidarity of the people in the struggle against imperialism and colonialism!"[183]

To a significant extent, such propagandizing reflected the anxieties of Khrushchev and other Soviet leaders about Castro's potential turn toward the Chinese. Peking castigated the Soviets as "revisionist" for their contention that peaceful coexistence between states with different social and economic systems did not preclude the triumph of socialist revolution.[184] A collapse of Moscow's position in the Caribbean would entail a major loss of Soviet prestige in the Third World. As early as March 1961, high-ranking members of the Cuban Communist Party had complained to the Kremlin about Che's support for armed revolutionary movements in the Western Hemisphere, and Castro's launch of a rebel training program in Havana was worrisome to Soviet leaders who feared another U.S. invasion of Cuba.[185] Castro's declaration in December 1961 that he was a Marxist-Leninist and sought to transform Cuba into a socialist country had complicated his domestic position, and Soviet intelligence

---

183. Text of the resolution adopted on April 17, 1961 by public representatives of Moscow at a meeting dedicated to Africa Freedom Day. AVPRF, F. 104, O. 16, P. 8, D. 9, Ll. 20–22.

184. Pavlov, *Soviet-Cuban Alliance*, p. 24.

185. Fursenko and Naftali, *One Hell of a Gamble*, pp. 140–141.

supported . . . the invasion of our country at the Bay of Pigs?"[193] He argued that the organization, in condemning Cuban aggression while failing to condemn U.S. aggression, was acting as a tool of the United States. Then, a few days after the meeting ended, Castro himself lashed back with a speech known as the Second Declaration of Havana, in which he denounced the Punta del Este meeting as a "consecration of the Yankees' odious right of intervention in the internal affairs of Latin America; the submission of the peoples entirely to the will of the United States of America."[194]

The Cubans, despite successfully repelling the U.S.-backed invasion, were not convinced that the United States had ceased efforts to destroy the revolution. On April 28, Castro and Dorticós penned a dire warning of impending U.S. aggression to Soviet foreign minister Andrei Gromyko. The revolutionary regime was now in danger of "direct armed aggression" from the United States and its band of counterrevolutionaries and mercenary thugs. Kennedy himself had "cynically acknowledged" the role of the U.S. government in the failed Bay of Pigs invasion, which "violated the most elementary norms of international law and the fundamental principles of the UN charter."[195] Castro and Dorticós absolved themselves of any responsibility for the breakdown in U.S.-Cuban relations, insisting that the revolutionary government had repeatedly announced its willingness to discuss "contentious issues" with the U.S. government "on a basis of equality." The United States had responded to these benevolent intentions with "threats of aggression and economic blockade, acts of sabotage and subversive activity, the bombardment of [Cuban] cities, and finally, the [Bay of Pigs] invasion." The United States was now bringing to bear its considerable military might against Cuba, "such a small country . . . which could never, even in a minor way, pose a threat or danger to such as great power as the U.S.A."[196]

The Cuban assessment of U.S. intentions to destroy the revolution was on the mark. Far from reevaluating its policy toward Cuba in the aftermath of the Bay of Pigs fiasco, the Kennedy administration instead

---

193. Quoted in Julio García Luis, ed., *Cuban Revolution Reader: A Documentary History of Fidel Castro's Revolution* (New York: Ocean Press, 2008), p. 126.

194. Quoted in ibid., p. 130–131.

195. Telegram to Soviet Foreign Minister Gromyko from Osvaldo Dorticós and Fidel Castro, April 28, 1961. AVPRF, F. 104, O. 16, P. 8, D. 9, L. 34.

196. Ibid., L. 35.

doubled down on hostilities, hoping in vain that the Castro regime could ultimately be replaced with one friendlier to the United States. In a report prepared mere days after the failed invasion, director of the Department of State's Policy Planning Staff Walt W. Rostow reiterated the ideological and military threats posed by the Soviet-Cuban alliance and recommended that the Organization of American States implement a selective blockade of Cuba in order to prevent arms shipments to the Castro regime.[197] Operation Mongoose was developed with the ultimate goal of shaping "the future of Cuba after the Castro government is overthrown."[198] The plan envisioned the continued support of Cuban exiles for an eventual invasion and regime change. Remarkably, even after the Bay of Pigs had revealed the dearth of U.S. intelligence on the actual conditions on the ground in Cuba, U.S. officials tasked with implementing Mongoose acknowledged, "We still know too little about the real situation inside Cuba."[199] Despite this lack of knowledge, and despite the fact that the Bay of Pigs disaster had revealed an unanticipated degree of Cuban support for Castro, Mongoose aimed to foment an internal rebellion against the Castro regime. Though the plan relied heavily on "indigenous resources," it projected that "final success will require decisive U.S. military intervention."[200] It would seem as though the only lesson Kennedy administration officials had learned from their mistakes was the difficulty of removing Castro absent an overt U.S. armed intervention. Kennedy himself, however, rejected the possibility of a U.S. military invasion out of hand. It is still not entirely clear how he expected to overthrow Castro in the event that the much-vaunted opposition forces failed to materialize, yet his appointment of his brother Robert F. Kennedy as head of Operation Mongoose demonstrated how personally invested he was in Cuban regime change.

---

197. "Memorandum from the President's Deputy Special Assistant for National Security Affairs (Rostow) to Secretary of Defense McNamara," April 24, 1961, *FRUS, 1961–1963, Volume X: Cuba, January 1961–September 1962*, Document 172, https://history.state.gov/historicaldocuments/frus1961-63v10/d172, accessed June 6, 2017.

198. "Minutes of first OPERATION MONGOOSE meeting with Attorney General Robert Kennedy," December 1, 1961, in Laurence Chang and Peter Kornbluh, eds., *The Cuban Missile Crisis: A National Security Archive Documents Reader* (New York: The New Press, 1992), p. 21.

199. Brig. Gen. Edward Lansdale, "The Cuba Project," February 20, 1962, in ibid., p. 23.

200. "Guidelines for OPERATION MONGOOSE," March 14, 1962, in ibid., p. 38.

of nuclear weaponry to Cuba as a response to U.S. and NATO's nuclear policy. Khrushchev recalls thinking that "the Americans had surrounded our country with military bases and threatened us with nuclear weapons, and now they would learn just what it feels like to have enemy missiles pointing at you; we'd be doing nothing more than giving them a little of their own medicine."[215] Though Kennedy had been elected on a hawkish foreign policy platform that decried the existence of a "missile gap" between the United States and the Soviet Union, we now know that any gap that existed was in the United States' favor. Indeed, at the time of the missile crisis, the United States enjoyed a seventeen-to-one advantage in strategic weaponry.[216] At no point during the Cold War did the Soviets ever exercise nuclear superiority over the United States. At the time, however, especially after the Soviet launch of Sputnik in 1957, it seemed that the USSR was poised to surpass the United States in the realm of science and technology. Khrushchev, of course, was well aware of Soviet strategic inferiority, and it was a situation he hoped to rectify. He believed that the installation of nuclear missiles in Cuba could bring the Soviet Union into a state of nuclear parity with the United States, and that this parity could potentially bring concrete strategic gains in the form of Western concessions on Berlin or in Southeast Asia.[217]

The situation in Berlin was complicated. The city had been divided into Soviet and American zones of influence, and the East Germans viewed West Berlin as a threat. This was because the residents of the Western zone enjoyed a much higher standard of living than did their counterparts in the East, so much so that it created a virtual flood of refugees fleeing from the East to the West. For the Soviets, this was a public relations disaster. How could they continue touting the glories of socialism when the example of East and West Germany demonstrated that so many people were willing to risk their lives to escape the Soviet zone? At the June 1961 summit in Vienna, Khrushchev had issued a demand to Kennedy: evacuate all Western troops from Berlin by the end of the year. Kennedy refused to bow to this order, and responded by building up military forces in the area. U.S. officials were well aware, however, that the Soviets enjoyed superiority in conventional forces in Europe, and

---

215. Strobe Talbott, ed., *Khrushchev Remembers* (Boston, MA: Little, Brown and Company, 1970), p. 494.

216. Gaddis, *We Now Know*, p. 262.

217. Dobrynin, *In Confidence*, p. 73.

Kennedy therefore seems to have believed that nuclear deterrence would prevent an armed conflict in Berlin.[218] In August 1961, the Soviets and East Germans reacted to the continued flow of refugees by constructing a wall to physically separate East and West Berlin. Kennedy was convinced that Khrushchev sought to use the improved Soviet strategic situation to force a Western withdrawal from Berlin.[219] Though this may have in fact occurred to some in the Kremlin, for Khrushchev it appeared to be a secondary consideration in his decision to station nuclear weapons in Cuba.[220]

There were, however, compelling ideological reasons for the Soviets to supply the Cubans with nuclear weaponry. The Cuban Revolution was the first time an avowedly Marxist-Leninist leader had come to power without foreign intervention or any meaningful assistance from the socialist bloc. The development of the Soviet-Cuban alliance, and the genuine warmth and enthusiasm shared by Castro and Khrushchev in the heady days of that burgeoning alliance, meant that Soviet leaders were sincerely concerned for the fate of the Cuban Revolution. The Bay of Pigs debacle had proven beyond the shadow of a doubt that the Kennedy administration would not rest until Castro had been overthrown. When Soviet leaders claimed that they were trying to help the Cuban Revolution survive the machinations of the great power of the North, they were sincere. The defense of the Castro regime was a key concern for Khrushchev.

There was another ideological aspect to the decision to launch Operation Anadyr, but it had less to do with the Cubans than with the Chinese. The Sino-Soviet split had by this time emerged publicly, with Mao challenging Khrushchev on a number of issues, including support for Third World allies. Mao envisioned the People's Republic of China as a more appropriate revolutionary model for the underdeveloped world

---

218. Graham Allison and Philip Zelikow, *Essence of Decision: Explaining the Cuban Missile Crisis*, 2nd ed. (New York: Longman, 1999), p. 101.

219. Ibid., p. 104.

220. In talks with the Cubans, Anastas Mikoyan claimed that Soviet requests to the Kennedy administration to resolve the Berlin issue were made as a "diversionary maneuver," and "in reality, we had no intention of resolving the Berlin question at that time." Memorandum of Conversation between Castro and Mikoyan, November 4, 1962, in Sergo Mikoyan, *The Soviet Cuban Missile Crisis: Castro, Mikoyan, Kennedy, Khrushchev, and the Missiles of November* (Washington, DC, and Stanford, CA: Woodrow Wilson Center Press and Stanford University Press, 2012), Document 8, p. 306.

conjecturing that he might want to provoke the United States into taking action against Cuba so that he could retaliate in Berlin.[231] There would be much speculation about Berlin in subsequent meetings.

In this first ExComm meeting, there was some debate over what Khrushchev's motivations were exactly. No one at this point suggested that the reason for stationing missiles on the island might actually be to defend Cuba against a U.S. invasion, which is especially surprising given that a Special National Intelligence Estimate drawn up in September had analyzed the Soviet military buildup in Cuba and concluded that its purpose was to "strengthen the Communist regime there against what the Cubans and the Soviets conceive to be a danger that the US may attempt by one means or another to overthrow it."[232] The intelligence estimate acknowledged that the Soviets could "derive considerable military advantage" from the emplacement of medium- and intermediate-range ballistic missiles in Cuba, but predicted that such a scenario was too risky for Soviet leaders to pursue.[233] This prediction obviously proved mistaken.

At the second ExComm meeting on October 16, Assistant Secretary of State for Inter-American Affairs Edwin Martin raised the issue of Cuban-Soviet relations and theorized that if Khrushchev was seeking to use the missiles to obtain a bargaining advantage in negotiations over Berlin, then Castro might realize "the way the Soviets are using him."[234] This would prove prophetic as the Cuban leadership was apoplectic at the way the Soviets bargained away their protection for what was considered a thoroughly useless guarantee from the Kennedy administration that it would not invade Cuba. Undersecretary of State George Ball also suggested that while Khrushchev may be looking to enhance Soviet strategic capabilities, it was also possible that "it is simply a trading ploy."[235] There was also some debate over just how much the strategic nuclear balance of power had changed as a result of Soviet weapons deliveries. At this point, the photographs had returned evidence only of medium-range

---

231. Transcript of first Executive Committee meeting, October 16, 1962, in Chang and Kornbluh, eds., *Cuban Missile Crisis*, p. 93.

232. Special National Security Intelligence Estimate, "The Military Buildup in Cuba," September 19, 1962, in ibid., p. 64.

233. Ibid., p. 65.

234. Transcript of second Executive Committee meeting, October 16, 1962, in ibid., p. 99.

235. Ibid., p. 106.

ballistic missile (MRBM) sites in Cuba, and though the Joint Chiefs of Staff reportedly believed that the strategic impact of the MRBMs was substantial, Defense Secretary McNamara thought the strategic situation had changed "not at all." Kennedy himself agreed with McNamara; after all, "they've got enough to blow us up now anyway," so "what difference does it make?"[236] Regardless of the strategic implications of the weapons systems, the members of the Executive Committee were unanimous in agreeing that these weapons could not be allowed to remain in Cuba. The blockade option was again discussed, with Joint Chiefs of Staff chairman Maxwell Taylor distinguishing between two types of blockade: one that stops ships from entering Cuban waters and one that simply searches those ships. National Security Adviser Bundy quickly realized the danger inherent in such a blockade: "You have to make the guy stop to search him, and if he won't stop, you have to shoot, right?"[237]

The following day, Special Counsel Theodore Sorensen drew up a summary of facts and premises and possible courses of action. It was generally agreed that even if the missiles were fully operational, they would not significantly modify the balance of power. The motivations of the Soviet leadership were also poorly understood. The possibilities raised—that it could be a diversionary tactic, a provocation, a means of harassment, or for the purpose of bargaining—did not include what Khrushchev then, and later claimed, was his primary motivation: protecting the Cuban Revolution against U.S. aggression.[238] The CIA asserted that the major Soviet objective was "to demonstrate that the world balance of forces has shifted so far in their favor that the US can no longer prevent the advance of Soviet offensive power even into its own hemisphere."[239] In this view, not only would the weapons systems augment Soviet strategic capabilities, but they would also have a profound psychological impact on U.S. leaders.

The Joint Chiefs of Staff were meanwhile working on plans for a ground invasion of Cuba. Believing that the sabotage campaign carried out under the auspices of Operation Mongoose was ineffective, the Joint

---

236. Ibid., p. 103.

237. Ibid., p. 111.

238. Theodore Sorensen, "Summary of Agreed Facts and Premises, Possible Courses of Action and Unanswered Questions," October 17, 1962, in ibid., p. 114.

239. CIA Special National Intelligence Estimate, "Major Consequences of Certain U.S. Courses of Action on Cuba," October 20, 1962, in ibid., p. 137.

Chiefs had been arguing for months that the U.S. armed forces should storm the island and remove Castro from power. Before the discovery of the Soviet missile construction sites, they had faced the problem of how to justify such an invasion. In an August 8 memorandum, the Joint Chiefs had suggested manufacturing an incident that could be used as a pretext for war, such as blowing up a U.S. ship in Guantánamo Bay and blaming it on Castro.[240] They were seemingly convinced that they could organize an attack on Cuba and keep the conflict localized to avoid an outbreak of hostilities with the Soviet Union. They predicted that a single infantry division would be adequate to occupy the island in the aftermath of Castro's overthrow. The Marine Corps was the only dissenting voice; believing that the Joint Chiefs' scenario underestimated Cuban resistance, they contended that at least three infantry divisions would be required to pacify the island. The Marine Corps had a better understanding of Cuban history, having occupied the country on and off since the Spanish-American War and witnessing firsthand the difficulties involved in restoring political and social stability.[241]

On October 18, more U-2 photos divulged evidence of the construction of sites to house intermediate-range ballistic missiles (IRBMs), which had twice the range of the MRBMs. The presence of the Soviet strategic bombers was also discovered. This revelation amplified the chorus calling for immediate air strikes on the missile sites, yet Kennedy cautiously refrained from taking any military action, instead tentatively suggesting the possibility of a trade involving the removal of the U.S. missiles from Turkey. Though many were still in favor of air strikes, there were powerful arguments against them. The Soviets could easily retaliate with strikes on U.S. or NATO bases in Berlin, Turkey, Iran, or any number of other locations. This situation could too quickly and easily escalate into an all-out nuclear war. Moreover, as Undersecretary of State Ball and others argued, a surprise attack would undermine U.S. moral standing and alienate allies. The sneak attack option was compared to the Japanese attack at Pearl Harbor, as a result of which "we tried the Japanese as war criminals."[242]

---

240. Dobbs, *One Minute to Midnight*, p. 17.

241. Ibid., pp. 18–19.

242. "Position of George W. Ball," in support of blockade option against Cuba, October 18, 1962, in Chang and Kornbluh, eds., *Cuban Missile Crisis*, p. 121.

Several of Kennedy's advisers were leaning more toward the blockade option at this point, which the president fervently hoped would not include a declaration of war. On October 19, Kennedy announced to the Joint Chiefs of Staff his decision to pursue the blockade. Air Force Chief of Staff General Curtis Lemay, who had pressed hard for a full-scale invasion of Cuba, compared Kennedy's decision to the appeasement of Adolf Hitler at Munich—a comparison that incurred shock and consternation from the other ExComm members.[243] Although Secretary of Defense Robert McNamara endorsed the blockade option, the chairman of the Joint Chiefs of Staff General Maxwell Taylor continued to insist that conducting air strikes on the missile sites would be far less dangerous than allowing them to become operational. Sorensen drafted an air strike scenario arguing that the strikes would have to hit the entire complex of weapons systems in Cuba—MRBMs, SAMs, high-performance aircraft, and nuclear storage sites. Because of the dangers inherent in any surviving Cuban air capability, "this build-up should be hit as a whole complex, or not at all."[244] Sorensen, however, was not necessarily in favor of air strikes, and he invoked the Pearl Harbor analogy, arguing that a U.S.-initiated sneak attack on a small country was something "which history could neither understand nor forget."[245] The consequences for U.S. moral superiority in the Cold War and in general would thus be profound. Kennedy was keenly aware of how quickly air strikes could escalate into all-out nuclear war and he ordered that the Jupiter missiles in Turkey were not to be fired without direct presidential order, even in the case of an unprovoked attack.

On October 20, the U.S. military adviser at the United Nations informed U.N. secretary-general U Thant's military adviser, General Indar Jit Rikhye, about the missiles. General Rikhye attended a secret briefing at the Pentagon and then reported back to Thant about what he had

---

243. JFK's father, Joseph P. Kennedy Sr., had been the U.S. ambassador to the United Kingdom at the time of the Munich conference, where UK prime minister Neville Chamberlain had infamously agreed to accept Hitler's annexation of portions of Czechoslovakia. The "appeasement" comparison hurled by LeMay thus had the feel of a personal attack on the Kennedy clan.

244. Theodore Sorensen, draft "Air Strike Scenario for October 19, 1962," in Chang and Kornbluh, eds., *Cuban Missile Crisis*, p. 128.

245. Theodore Sorensen, "Summary of Objections to Air Strike Option and Advantages of Blockade Option," October 20, 1962, in ibid., p. 133.

Figure 7. This was one of the first U-2 photographs shown
to Kennedy on October 16, 1962. It depicts a medium-range
ballistic missile site under construction in San Cristóbal,
Cuba. (Central Intelligence Agency/public domain)

"piratical measures, the kind that were practiced in the Middle Ages."[265] He
suggested that if the United States would shut down the quarantine and
pledge not to invade Cuba, he would declare that the ships bound for Cuba
had no armaments aboard. On October 27, the CIA reported that the four
MRBM sites at San Cristóbal and the two sites at Sagua La Grande had
become fully operational. Cuban military forces were continuing to mobi-
lize rapidly, and the six Soviet and three socialist bloc vessels en route to
Cuba had not changed course. A Swedish vessel that was believed to be
chartered by the USSR had been allowed to proceed to Havana despite
refusing to stop when intercepted by a U.S. destroyer.[266]

---

265. Khrushchev letter to Kennedy, October 26, 1962, in Chang and Kornbluh, eds.,
Cuban Missile Crisis, p. 186.

266. CIA Daily Report, "The Crisis USSR/Cuba," October 27, 1962, in ibid., p. 195.

Figure 8. This photograph, depicting a second medium-range ballistic missile launch site in San Cristóbal, Cuba, was presented to Kennedy on November 1, 1962, after a deal had been worked out with Khrushchev to withdraw all offensive weaponry but before verification procedures had been agreed upon. (Central Intelligence Agency/public domain)

The same day, in Oriente province, an American U-2 spy plane was shot down, instantly killing the pilot, Major Rudolf Anderson. The day before, Castro had ordered his troops to fire at any plane that traversed Cuban airspace, but the surface-to-air missiles were ostensibly under Soviet command. General Issa Pliyev had put the Soviet SAMs on full alert and cabled Moscow for permission to fire at any U.S. planes flying over Soviet installation sites. Moscow had not yet replied to this request when the U-2 was shot down. Lieutenant General Stepan Grechko, the Soviet air defense commander in Cuba, presumably issued the order to fire at the U-2.[267] The assumption was that the Americans had initiated combat and that this turn of events overruled prior restrictions on the

---

267. Taubman, *Khrushchev*, p. 571.

told the ambassador, "I haven't seen my children for days now, and the President hasn't seen his either. We're spending all day and night at the White House; I don't know how much longer we can hold out against our generals."[284] Khrushchev apparently later claimed that this conversation was the "culminating point of the crisis," when the tide in Moscow was turned away from war and toward a peaceful solution.[285]

Khrushchev replied the following day, assuring the president that he had "issued a new order on the dismantling of the weapons which you describe as 'offensive,' and their crating and return to the Soviet Union."[286] He also agreed to allow U.N. inspectors to verify that the weapons were removed. This would prove contentious for Castro, who would later deny permission to U.N. inspectors to enter Cuban territory. The wording of the letter proved important, as Khrushchev essentially granted the Kennedy administration the right to define "offensive" versus "defensive" weapons. A debate over precisely that definition erupted, and was only resolved after weeks of negotiations under the auspices of the United Nations. Though Khrushchev's acceptance of Kennedy's terms ended the most dangerous phase of the crisis, there were several unresolved issues that would bedevil Soviet relations with both Cuba and the United States.

Crisis Dénouement: The Missiles of November

Among the issues that continued to forestall a final settlement was exactly which weapons were to be removed from Cuban territory. There was some disagreement over how to define "offensive" versus "defensive" weapons systems, not only among the Americans and the Soviets, but also within the Kennedy administration itself. State Department officials argued that the surface-to-surface missiles and the IL-28 light jet bombers were the only clearly offensive weapons, and while the administration should propose that short-range coastal defense missiles and short-range artillery rockets also be removed, they should be excluded if the Soviets

---

284. Quoted in Talbott, *Khrushchev Remembers*, p. 498.

285. Dobrynin, *In Confidence*, p. 88.

286. Premier Khrushchev's communiqué to President Kennedy, accepting an end to the missile crisis, October 28, 1962, in Chang and Kornbluh, eds., *Cuban Missile Crisis*, p. 226.

put up a fuss. State believed that it would be unreasonable to request the removal of the MiG fighters, surface-to-air missiles, and non-missile ground force weapons.[287]

Perhaps the most contentious issue, from Castro's perspective, was that the Soviet premier had not even deigned to inform him, much less consult him, about the terms of the agreement. Only after Khrushchev accepted Kennedy's terms did he bother to let Castro know what they were. In a letter to Castro, Khrushchev claimed that the crisis had been resolved "in your favor," as Kennedy had agreed that his administration would cease its attempts to destroy the Cuban Revolution. Khrushchev implored Castro "not to be carried away by sentiment," and assured him that he understood the Cuban leader's "indignation" toward the United States.[288] In conversations with Soviet officials in Havana, Castro revealed the deep discontent of the Cuban people, who were "consumed by a sense of disappointment, confusion, and bitterness" over the withdrawal of the missiles, which they apparently believed had become Cuban property.[289]

Upon discovering that Khrushchev and Kennedy had reached a deal, Castro issued five conditions under which he himself would consider the crisis resolved. He demanded the immediate termination of the U.S. economic blockade, the cessation of all subversive activities and "piratical attacks" against Cuba from U.S. bases, respect for Cuban airspace and territorial waters, and the evacuation of the U.S. naval base at Guantánamo. Castro also pointedly refused to allow on-site inspection to verify the withdrawal of the missiles and bombers, unless Cuba was granted the right to inspect U.S. facilities in South Florida where the CIA trained Cuban exiles.[290] Nor would Castro permit aerial surveillance, even by the United Nations, viewing it as a violation of Cuban sovereignty. The Cuban leader was reportedly "furious" with Khrushchev for his verification commitment, and refused to even allow inspection of the

---

287. State Department memorandum, "Considerations in Defining Weapons Which Must be Removed from Cuba," October 29, 1962, in ibid., p. 247.

288. Premier Khrushchev's letter to Prime Minister Castro, informing him of a deal to withdraw the missiles, October 28, 1962, in ibid., p. 239.

289. "Notes of Conversation between A. I. Mikoyan and Fidel Castro," November 3, 1961, in Mikoyan, *The Soviet Cuban Missile Crisis*, Document 6, pp. 295–296.

290. Blight, *Cuba on the Brink*, p. 23.

sites after they have been dismantled and evacuated.[291] Castro would not budge on this issue. He invoked the Platt Amendment as an example of the intolerable limits placed on Cuban sovereignty by the U.S. government, and emphatically declared that inspections would be akin to permitting the United States "to determine what we can or cannot do in foreign policy."[292] After an acrimonious exchange of letters between Khrushchev and Castro, with the Soviet premier insisting that he had consulted with the Cuban leader on the deal reached with the United States, Anastas Mikoyan was dispatched to Havana on November 2 to assure the Cubans that the primary goal of stationing the missiles had been achieved—the Kennedy administration had pledged not to invade Cuba.[293] Mikoyan, a consummate diplomat, had been the first high-ranking Soviet official to visit Cuba after the triumph of the revolution, and the Cubans implicitly trusted him, especially after he refused to return to Moscow to attend the funeral of his wife, who died right after Mikoyan landed in Havana. The grieving Soviet diplomat's insistence on remaining in Havana to work things out with the Cubans made a powerful impression on Castro.

While negotiations between the USSR and Cuba continued at the bilateral level, negotiations between the Soviets and the Americans proceeded under the auspices of the United Nations. The most pressing issues concerned the weapons to be removed and the inspection procedures for verifying their removal. Secretary General U Thant felt personally invested in a peaceful outcome to the crisis and traveled to Cuba at the end of October to meet with Castro personally. Castro was still furious, and rejected Thant's proposal to station U.N. personnel on the island to liaise between himself and the Cuban leader. Though Thant implored Castro to allow the United Nations to supervise the dismantling of the missile sites, Castro refused, protesting that it would be an unacceptable violation of Cuban sovereignty.[294]

U.S. secretary of state Dean Rusk insisted that the United States continue aerial overflights of Cuban territory, even though the SAM sites

---

291. State Department cable on U.N. secretary-general U Thant's meetings with Prime Minister Castro, November 1, 1962, in Chang and Kornbluh, eds., *Cuban Missile Crisis*, p. 249.

292. Memorandum of Conversation between Castro and Mikoyan, November 4, 1962, in Mikoyan, *The Soviet Cuban Missile Crisis*, Document 8, p. 303.

293. Fursenko and Naftali, *One Hell of a Gamble*, pp. 293–294.

294. Dorn and Pauk, "Unsung Mediator," p. 285.

on the island were already operational. He hoped that the Cubans and Russians would agree to allow the overflights.[295] Given Castro's vehement refusal to allow any overflights, much less those conducted by U.S. U-2s, this was a vain hope. And yet the U-2 reconnaissance missions continued and were not obstructed. Chairman of the Joint Chiefs of Staff General Maxwell Taylor argued that the Kennedy administration should withhold publicly promising not to invade Cuba until Castro accepted continued U.S. air surveillance.[296] Taylor was extremely hawkish in defining which weapons were offensive and should be removed—he also viewed the SAM sites, the MiGs, the air defense control system, and the "large stocks of modern Army equipment" as problematic. He argued that not only would they interfere with U.S. aerial reconnaissance, but also "may be used against Guantanamo or against any invasion attempt."[297] This demonstrates that regardless of President Kennedy's non-invasion pledge, U.S. military commanders had not ruled out a future invasion of Cuba.

The IL-28 light bombers were a major point of contention, with Kennedy administration officials arguing that they must be removed and Khrushchev countering that these were already obsolete and not for offensive purposes. Both sides had a point. Technological advances had rendered the IL-28s outdated at best, and yet they were still capable of carrying nuclear weapons and delivering them to targets in the continental United States. As long as the IL-28s remained in Cuba, the Kennedy administration refused to dismantle the naval quarantine. Khrushchev argued that since the MRBMs and IRBMs had already been shipped back to the Soviet bloc, it was incumbent upon the United States to immediately call an end to the quarantine and to cease violating Cuban territorial waters and airspace.[298] Additionally, Khrushchev addressed concerns about the offensive potential of the IL-28s, emphasizing that they would only be piloted by Soviet, and never Cuban, personnel. Nevertheless, to further assuage U.S. officials,

---

295. Bromley Smith, "Summary Record of NSC Executive Committee Meeting," November 5, 1962, in Change and Kornbluh, eds., Cuban Missile Crisis, p. 263.

296. General Maxwell Taylor, "Chairman's Talking Paper for Meeting with the President," November 16, 1962, in ibid., p. 281.

297. Ibid., p. 280.

298. Premier Khrushchev's letter to President Kennedy, November 11, 1962, in ibid., p. 270.

Khrushchev later rescinded Pliyev's authority to employ tactical nukes in the event of a U.S. invasion of Cuba, on October 26, Pliyev, anticipating an imminent U.S. attack, ordered a number of nuclear warheads transported to rockets for emplacement. Soviet defense minister General Rodion Malinovsky cabled back to Pliyev on October 27, explicitly forbidding him or anyone else from employing any nuclear weapons without express authorization from Moscow.[318]

According to Anastas Mikoyan, after Kennedy announced the blockade, Malinovsky proposed that command of the missile batteries be handed over to the Cuban military. Khrushchev apparently found the idea appealing, as it would effectively remove the Soviets from the crisis, and the Americans would have to negotiate directly with the Cubans. Mikoyan himself strenuously objected to the proposal, on the grounds that the Kennedy administration would never come to terms with a nuclear-armed Cuba, and that to put the weapons in Castro's hands would endanger the entire human race. Khrushchev seems to have understood the logic, and he ultimately rejected Malinovsky's proposal.[319] Given the immensity of what was at stake in the crisis, and the overwhelming responsibility that was placed on individuals who not only lacked full knowledge of the situation, but were also quite human and subject to all manner of human foibles, vanities, and miscalculations, it should hardly come as a surprise that the world came within a hair's breadth of annihilation.

Nuclear Fallout: Consequences of the Missile Crisis

In the immediate aftermath of the crisis, Khrushchev and other Soviet leaders, as well as pro-Soviet politicians in Latin America and elsewhere, attempted to portray the outcome as a victory for the USSR. Soviet diplomats were tasked with assuring doubters that what the Soviets called "the Caribbean crisis" (because to refer to it as the "missile crisis" would be tantamount to admitting that it was Khrushchev's decision to launch Operation Anadyr that had provoked the crisis in the first place) had "ended in a total victory for the USSR." These claims to victory were

---

318. Ibid., p. 63.

319. Mikoyan, *The Soviet Cuban Missile Crisis*, p. 148.

founded on the belief that the Kennedy administration's non-invasion pledge would "not allow the United States to subjugate Latin America as in the past."[320] Given that the Kennedy administration had clearly not abandoned its efforts to unseat Castro, this was a dubious claim indeed, though it should be noted that subsequent U.S. presidents did abide by Kennedy's pledge not to launch another overt invasion of the island.

In reality, the outcome of the missile crisis was a veritable disaster for the USSR. Not only did it contribute to Khrushchev's ouster from power two years later, but Soviet credibility among its Third World allies was shaken, and the incident incurred the wrath of Fidel Castro, inaugurating a deep freeze in the Cuban-Soviet relationship. Despite Soviet claims that the Cuban Revolution had been safeguarded by Kennedy's non-invasion pledge, the missile crisis did not provoke a major re-conceptualization of U.S. policy toward Cuba. The Kennedy administration continued to pursue covert measures to destabilize the Castro regime, in the hopes of creating an atmosphere conducive to the ultimate overthrow of Castro and his replacement with a ruling regime friendlier to the United States. As early as January 1963, Kennedy warned the members of the National Security Council that "the time will probably come when we will have to act again on Cuba," and when that time arrived, it was imperative "to be ready to move with all possible speed."[321] As two historians of the crisis have put it, "the latitude to overthrow Castro . . . was more important than a concrete resolution to the most dangerous international crisis of the twentieth century."[322]

Cuban officials were well aware of continued U.S. aggressive intentions, and in March 1963, Cuban foreign minister Raúl Roa sent U.N. secretary-general U Thant a letter of protest. Citing the openly hostile statements of several U.S. administration officials and congressmen, Roa maintained, "Those directly and indirectly responsible for U.S. foreign policy do not conceal their violations of the U.N. Charter or their desire

---

320. Soviet embassy in Syria, memorandum of conversation with Chilean chargé d'affaires in Syria and Lebanon Carlos Dimer, January 16, 1963. AVPRF, F. 139, O. 18, P. 3, D. 1, L. 2.

321. "Notes of President Kennedy's Remarks at the 508th Meeting of the National Security Council, January 22, 1963, *FRUS, 1961–1963*, Volume XI: Cuban Missile Crisis and Aftermath, Document 271, permanent URL: https://history.state.gov /historicaldocuments/frus1961-63v11/d271, accessed August 11, 2017.

322. Chang and Kornbluh, eds., *Cuban Missile Crisis*, p. 236.

to destroy a Member State."[323] Reflecting the disdain of the Cuban leadership for the Organization of American States, Roa argued that several member countries had presented false information to the regional security forum about Cuban-sponsored hemispheric subversion. "Since the Punta del Este meeting," he charged, these countries had coalesced into "an aggressive military block serving U.S. imperialism."[324] Roa warned that if the United Nations failed to respond adequately to Cuban complaints of the aggressive actions of the United States, it too would be revealed as a tool of U.S. imperialism.

Indeed, the outcome of the missile crisis showed that, for all the attempts by Secretary General U Thant to mediate the conflict, the superpowers would continue to act unilaterally to defend their perceived interests, even when such actions directly contravened both the spirit and the letter of the U.N. charter. U Thant, despite his active efforts at mediating the crisis, and despite the fact that his efforts clearly bore fruit, understood this to be the case. A few months after the resolution of the crisis, he acknowledged, "The United Nations cannot overawe the nuclear powers."[325]

The consequences of the missile crisis extended to the political power and leadership of Nikita Khrushchev himself. The Kremlin plotters who masterminded the "palace coup" that ousted Khrushchev cited the missile crisis as the most blatant example of the Soviet premier's reckless adventurism. Presidium member Dmitry Polyanski, who delivered a scathing indictment of Khrushchev's leadership, invited the deposed premier to "ask any one of our marshals or generals, and they will tell you that plans for the military 'penetration' of South America were gibberish, fraught with the enormous danger of war."[326] During the Presidium session in which Khrushchev was effectively removed from power, Polyanski charged that the crisis had diminished the prestige of the Soviet Union

---

323. "Cuban Protest to the United Nations," letter from Cuban Foreign Minister Raúl Roa to UN Secretary General U Thant, March 4, 1963 (Havana, Cuba: Ministry of Foreign Relations, 1963), p. 12.

324. Ibid., p. 20.

325. U Thant quoted in Bernard J. Firestone, *The United Nations under U Thant, 1961–1971* (Lanham, MD: Scarecrow Press, 2001), p. 16.

326. Quoted in Blight and Brenner, *Sad and Luminous Days*, p. 353.

while bolstering the authority of the United States.[327] One former Soviet diplomat recalls, "Of all the international conflicts that erupted during the decade of Khrushchev's rule, the Cuban Missile Crisis . . . damaged his authority the most."[328] Khrushchev was chided for losing sight of Soviet security interests, which his successors argued must always be paramount in policy decisions.

Though the KGB and the International Department of the CPSU Central Committee would continue to support Third World national liberation movements, Leonid Brezhnev, Khrushchev's successor, took a more cautious approach to foreign policy.[329] The Brezhnev era witnessed a reorientation of Soviet foreign policy away from the revolutionary adventurism of the Khrushchev era and toward a more pragmatic calculus of Soviet security interests. This reflects the degree to which the Cuban fiasco was the product of Khrushchev's own mercurial adventurism, for which he paid a high price. The outcome of the crisis led to a humiliating public defeat for the Soviets and constituted a serious blow to Moscow's international prestige and its image in the Third World. The Soviet military parlayed the humiliating experience into the development of a dramatically expanded nuclear arsenal.[330] This effort to correct the strategic imbalance and improve Moscow's strategic position would include a buildup of ICBM forces, so that, in the words of the Soviet deputy foreign minister, "You Americans will never be able to do this to us again."[331]

There was another area in which the Soviets benefited from the outcome of the crisis. Relations with the United States would never again deteriorate to the point of a near declaration of war. The back channel diplomacy of Robert Kennedy and Anatoly Dobrynin would continue

---

327. Aleksandr Fursenko and Timothy Naftali, "Soviet Intelligence and the Cuban Missile Crisis," in James G. Blight and David A. Welch, eds., *Intelligence and the Cuban Missile Crisis* (Portland, OR: Frank Cass Publishers, 1998), p. 64.

328. Victor Israelyan, *On the Battlefields of the Cold War: A Soviet Ambassador's Confession* (University Park: Pennsylvania State University Press, 2003), p. 75.

329. This cautious approach would later be abandoned with the Soviet invasion of Afghanistan in 1979.

330. Dobrynin, *In Confidence*, p. 93.

331. Quoted in Marc Trachtenberg, *History and Strategy* (Princeton, NJ: Princeton University Press, 1991), p. 257.

through other channels in future administrations.[332] On August 30, 1963, a "hot line" was established that provided a direct connection between the White House and the Kremlin to ensure that in any ensuing crisis situation, communications between U.S. and Soviet leaders would be unambiguous and instantaneous. Having peered into the nuclear abyss, both sides were painfully aware that the fate of humanity rested on their ability to ease tensions in the superpower relationship. Also in 1963, Washington and Moscow signed a limited nuclear test ban treaty, which prohibited all detonations of nuclear weapons for testing purposes, except for underground tests. Although the negotiations had initially centered on a more comprehensive nuclear test ban, Soviet concerns about verification procedures and technical issues involved in the detection of underground tests ultimately sunk the negotiations. While the signing of even a partial test ban treaty may seem like a significant achievement, in reality the ban did not halt the arms race, or even slow it down. It did, however, ease tensions between the United States and the Soviet Union, and lead to a series of other measures designed to reduce the proliferation of nuclear weapons.[333]

The Future of Cuban-Soviet Relations

The Cuban Missile Crisis was a watershed in the Cuban-Soviet relationship. It undermined Cuban trust in the Soviet leadership and led to a breach in the alliance that would not be repaired until the early 1970s. On October 29, after Castro discovered that Khrushchev had reached an agreement without even bothering to consult him, Soviet ambassador in Havana Aleksandr Alekseev cabled Moscow with the news that he had "never seen him [Castro] so distraught and irate."[334] The Cuban people were reportedly engaging in spontaneous anti-Soviet demonstrations throughout the country, ripping down pro-Soviet posters and

---

332. For more on back channel diplomacy, see Richard A. Moss, *Nixon's Back Channel to Moscow: Confidential Diplomacy and Détente* (Lexington: University Press of Kentucky, 2017).

333. For more, see James Hubert McBride, *The Test Ban Treaty: Military, Technological, and Political Implications* (Chicago: Henry Regnery, 1967).

334. Mikoyan, *The Soviet Cuban Missile Crisis*, p. 179.

billboards, and, at Castro's urging, chanting slurs that called into question Khrushchev's manhood.[335]

The missile crisis was the first serious rupture in the Cuban-Soviet alliance. Castro felt that Khrushchev had sold out the Cuban Revolution in order to gain Washington's favor. Indeed, in negotiations with Kennedy, Khrushchev falsified information so as to place the blame squarely on the Cubans; he claimed that the missiles were sent "per request of the Cuban government."[336] The crisis was a major breach in the Soviet-Cuban relationship; the level of trust and understanding that existed before the crisis would never again be reached. The Cubans had viewed the Soviet proposal to station missiles on Cuban territory as a form of protection tantamount to that given to the socialist bloc; in other words, the Cubans thought they were safely situated under the Soviet nuclear umbrella. Moreover, the Cubans believed that in safeguarding the revolution, the Soviets had tacitly agreed to Cuban support of armed revolutionary movements in the Western Hemisphere. In a single stroke, the Soviet capitulation to U.S. demands disabused the Cuban leadership of these notions. What made the reality particularly disillusioning is that the Cubans had been prepared to lay down their lives as martyrs to the revolutionary cause in the event of a nuclear war.[337] Though the alliance soldiered on until the end of the Cold War and the collapse of the USSR, the Cubans would never again trust the Soviets completely. Lev Mendelevich, the former chief of the Latin American Directorate of the Soviet Foreign Ministry, has been quoted as saying that "after what happened in 1962, the Cubans will never be our real friends."[338]

Nevertheless, Khrushchev was determined to repair relations with Castro, and in January 1963, sent him a long, rambling letter that included an invitation to Moscow and a thinly veiled warning against the provocations of the Chinese. The Chinese were quick to criticize Khrushchev, not only for the "venturesome blunder" of installing missiles in Cuba, but also because by removing the missiles, he had "capitulated to American imperialism."[339] With the Sino-Soviet split deepening, Havana looked to

---

335. Blight and Brenner, *Sad and Luminous Days*, p. 25.

336. Mikoyan, *The Soviet Cuban Missile Crisis*, p. 211.

337. Blight and Brenner, *Sad and Luminous Days*, pp. 74–75.

338. Quoted in Pavlov, *Soviet-Cuban Alliance*, p. 55.

339. *Jenmin Jibao* (Peking), quoted in ibid., p. 56.

Peking for ideological camaraderie and support to balance its dependence on Moscow.[340] Khrushchev sought to forestall any further strengthening of Sino-Cuban friendship, and believed that by spending time with Castro, he could convince the Cuban leader to realign with the Soviet party line. He pointed out, moreover, without naming China specifically, that "the leaders of certain socialist countries . . . did not take any step— verbal or material—that would have demonstrated their willingness to aid Cuba, to march with her if war broke out."[341]

Castro also expressed his disappointment that Khrushchev, while making voluntary concessions that had not been demanded by U.S. negotiators, had not pressed harder for concessions in Cuba's favor. That the Soviets did not even deign to keep Castro apprised of the negotiations, much less include the Cuban leadership in those negotiations, was a clear demonstration that when push came to shove, the USSR would act more as a Cold War superpower than as an anti-imperialist guarantor of Third World interests. In January 1968, Castro delivered his own "secret speech" to the Central Committee of the Cuban Communist Party. He admitted that in the period prior to the missile crisis, the Cuban leadership had put "tremendous faith in the Soviet Union . . . perhaps too much."[342]

Castro was surprised to learn that Khrushchev had secured a secret deal with Kennedy to remove ballistic missiles from Italy and Turkey in exchange for the withdrawal of Soviet missiles from Cuba. In fact, Castro was never supposed to find about the quid pro quo, but Khrushchev accidentally let it slip while reading a letter aloud to a translator in Castro's presence. Castro was surprised and dismayed; in his own words, "withdrawing the missiles from Turkey was in total contradiction to the theory that the essential goal had been the defense of Cuba."[343] Castro also later claimed that he had repeatedly asked several members of the Politburo what the strategic rationale for stationing missiles in Cuba was, but never received a straight answer.[344] Khrushchev did not even broach the issue

---

340. Lévesque, *The USSR and the Cuban Revolution*, p. 44.

341. Premier Khrushchev's letter to Prime Minister Castro, reviewing the crisis, January 31, 1963, in Chang and Kornbluh, eds., *Cuban Missile Crisis*, p. 320.

342. Blight and Brenner, *Sad and Luminous Days*, p. 35.

343. Foreign Broadcast Information Service, transcript of Fidel Castro's remarks at the Havana conference on the Cuban missile crisis, January 11, 1992, in Chang and Kornbluh, eds., *Cuban Missile Crisis*, p. 344.

344. Ibid., p. 336.

of terminating the U.S. lease on Guantánamo, nor did he request the cessation of U-2 flights over Cuban territory. Had Khrushchev at least obtained these concessions, Castro argued, the missile crisis "might even have been turned into a political victory." Instead, Khrushchev gave away the store, got virtually nothing in return, and the outcome of the entire episode was "an evident defeat for the socialist community and for the revolutionary movement."[345] Moreover, while the Soviet premier had assured his American counterparts that the weapons were sent at the request of the Cubans, in a letter to Castro he acknowledged, "We decided to propose the installation of the weapons."[346] And while the Soviet party line promulgated throughout the world was that the socialist camp had achieved a great victory in forcing the Kennedy administration to respect the sovereignty of Cuba, he privately admitted to Castro that "North American imperialism will not renounce its plans to end the socialist regime in Cuba, to abolish the revolutionary order in your country, and to restore capitalism and reaction there."[347]

For the Cubans, ultimately, the missile crisis was "the moment when the dream that one of the superpowers might help to foster a global revolution disappeared."[348] The Soviets, for their part, walked away from the missile crisis with a view of the Cubans as reckless, hotheaded, and intransigent. They believed that the Cubans had a martyr complex and that they had pushed the world to the brink of nuclear holocaust with their intemperance and unrealistic demands.[349] Indeed, Soviet propaganda insisted that it was Castro who had requested the missiles, and portrayed the Cubans as driving the Soviets to the brink of nuclear war.[350] These visions would never really go away, and the subsequent history of Cuban-Soviet relations would be plagued by Cuban distrust of Soviet "bureaucratism" and Soviet wariness of Cuban impetuousness. After the end of the Cold War, Jorge Pollo, a staff member of the Central Committee of the Cuban Communist Party, remarked, "History has

---

345. Blight and Brenner, *Sad and Luminous Days*, p. 67.

346. Premier Khrushchev's letter to Prime Minister Castro, reviewing the crisis, January 31, 1963, in Chang and Kornbluh, eds., *Cuban Missile Crisis*, p. 323.

347. Ibid., p. 325.

348. Blight and Brenner, *Sad and Luminous Days*, p. 84.

349. Ibid., p. 85.

350. Israelyan, *On the Battlefields of the Cold War*, p. 76.

Figure 12. A Soviet propaganda poster that reads, "Long live the eternal, unbreakable friendship and partnership between the Soviet and Cuban peoples!" (Photo by Keizers/CC BY-SA 3.0)

yet to record whether Cuba has suffered more from U.S. imperialism or Soviet friendship."[351]

For Castro, meanwhile, the outcome of the missile crisis imparted an even greater urgency to the revolutionary struggle in the hemisphere. The cultivation of Third World allies became more important as he faced both U.S. hostility and the inadequacy of Soviet protection. Fomenting revolutionary movements in Latin American and Africa would also force the United States into the sort of imperial overstretch envisioned by Che Guevara when he called for "two, three, many Vietnams." Additionally, the internationalism of the revolution would boost Cuban morale, which had suffered a grave defeat in the missile crisis.[352]

The Cuban leadership viewed its support for revolutionary movements in the Western Hemisphere as critical to Cuban national security, which was constantly threatened by real or imagined U.S. aggression.

---

351. Quoted in Blight and Brenner, *Sad and Luminous Days*, p. 93.

352. Ibid., p. 87.

Though the Cubans had never toed the "peaceful coexistence" line, after the missile crisis they viewed it as a fundamental betrayal of Third World interests and shorthand for the imperialist collusion that had sold out the Cuban Revolution.[353] That the Soviets and the Cubans drew such conflicting lessons from the missile crisis inevitably put them on a collision course.

Castro's support for revolutionary movements in Latin America had been a source of tension in the Cuban-Soviet relationship even before the missile crisis. Such support directly contradicted the CPSU line, which asserted that peaceful coexistence did not preclude socialist revolution, and that the best way to achieve the latter was through the concerted efforts of regional communist parties. On May 23, 1963, Castro and Khrushchev worked out a theoretical compromise on the issue of armed struggle. A joint communiqué stated that "the question of the peaceful or non-peaceful road to socialism in one country or another will be definitely decided by the struggling peoples themselves."[354] Orthodox communist parties interpreted this theoretical shift as a confirmation of their nonviolent tactics, but Castro seems to have interpreted it as an endorsement of revolutionary violence, because the next year he was back to trumpeting the "inevitability" of the armed struggle.[355]

Throughout the remainder of the 1960s, Cuban-Soviet relations would be constantly plagued by the contradiction between Castro's obligations as Soviet ally and his aspirations for Third World leadership. This manifested most frequently as criticism of orthodox communist parties; sometimes this criticism was thinly veiled, and other times it was direct and harsh. While adhering to the view that Yankee imperialism was the ultimate enemy, Castro consistently chastised both the Soviets and their regional communist allies for their inadequate support of the armed revolutionaries battling the imperialists.

In sum, the missile crisis had ruptured the Cuban-Soviet alliance and exposed the reality of Soviet great-power predilections, proving that in times of crisis, Moscow would have no qualms about sacrificing the goals and interests of its Third World allies to the necessity of maintaining cooperative relations with the United States. Though ultimately the

---

353. Ibid., p. 96.

354. D. Bruce Jackson, *Castro, the Kremlin, and Communism in Latin America* (Baltimore: Johns Hopkins University Press, 1969), p. 21.

355. Ibid., p. 22.

breach was repaired and the Cubans became consistent defenders of the Soviet Union in the United Nations and the Non-Aligned Movement, this was reflective more of Castro's unwillingness to antagonize his revolution's patrons in a changed situation of Cuban economic dependence on the USSR. Moreover, as the Cuban leadership subordinated its support for armed revolutionary movements to more traditional diplomatic and political engagement with the countries of Latin America, Cuba was reintegrated into the inter-American community and Soviet-Cuban relations improved dramatically.

Latin American Responses to the Missile Crisis

The crisis had profound consequences for Latin American regional relations. Before the stationing of Soviet missiles on Cuban soil, U.S. warnings about the threat Cuba posed to other countries of the hemisphere were not as credible as they were in the post-crisis atmosphere. The Cuban Missile Crisis revealed Cuban-Soviet machinations as an existential threat to the entire Western Hemisphere. On October 23, 1962—the day after Kennedy's and Castro's speeches to their respective nations about the crisis—the Organization of American States convened an emergency session to discuss hemispheric responses. The final draft of the OAS resolution was subjected to a section-by-section vote, and the delegations from Brazil, Bolivia, and Mexico abstained on the section authorizing the use of armed force in Cuba, though they did vote for the resolution as a whole. Thus, for the record, there was total unanimity on the vote.[356] The final resolution called for the immediate withdrawal of all Soviet missiles from Cuban territory and recommended "all measures," including the use of armed force in order to ensure that all offensive weapons were removed and that the Cuban government would not be able to receive any more military materiel from the Soviets.[357] As one scholar of Cuban foreign policy has argued, the OAS sanctions imparted a veneer of legitimacy to U.S. efforts to isolate Cuba from its neighbors in the Western

---

356. Jerome Slater, *The OAS and United States Foreign Policy* (Columbus: Ohio State University Press, 1967), p. 163.

357. O. Carlos Stoetzer, *The Organization of American States* (Westport, CT: Praeger, 1993), p. 281.

Hemisphere, destroy its economy, and ultimately to overthrow Castro.[358] Some Latin American countries were prepared to do more than merely affirm a U.S. draft resolution in the Organization of American States. Venezuela mobilized its armed forces, Argentina deployed warships to support the U.S. naval quarantine, and Brazil notified Moscow that its air force would inspect and remove cargo from any Soviet aircraft that stopped in Brazilian territory on the way to Havana.[359]

The aftermath of the missile crisis inspired a myriad of responses across the hemisphere. These responses were contingent not only upon a country's domestic politics, but upon the nature of its relations with both the United States and Cuba. Castro had made many enemies with his attempts to export the revolution, and these enemies pressured the United States to adopt a more belligerent stance. The Caribbean strongmen—targets of Cuban subversion—hoped to use the opportunity presented by the crisis to overthrow Castro. Not surprisingly, some countries located in close geographical proximity to Cuba expressed alarm about the nuclear missile sites and firmly supported U.S. efforts—including, if necessary, a full-scale military invasion—to remove them. According to the CIA, all six Central American countries, along with Argentina, the Dominican Republic, Paraguay, and Venezuela, favored "strong measures to eliminate the Castro regime," with Bolivia, Brazil, Chile, Mexico, and Uruguay opposed to any intervention in Cuba's internal affairs.[360] Although the Mexican delegation to the Organization of American States had rejected the use of armed force to remove the offensive weaponry, Mexican president Adolfo López Mateos, normally a public advocate for Castro, personally opposed the presence of Soviet missiles in Cuba.

While Latin American governments virtually united around the demand to remove the nukes from Cuban territory, Latin American publics reacted differently. Mass demonstrations of citizens in cities across the hemisphere took to the streets to protest U.S. actions and express sympathy with Castro. These protestors argued that Castro had every right to defend

358. Domínguez, *To Make a World Safe for Revolution*, pp. 28–29.

359. Renata Keller, "The Latin American Missile Crisis," *Diplomatic History* Vol. 39, No. 2 (April 2015), pp. 202, 205, and 217.

360. CIA, Office of Current Intelligence Memorandum, Subject: Attitude of Latin American Governments on Survival of Castro Cuba, November 20, 1962, National Security Country File, Cuba, Box 49, Folder: Cuba, Subjects, Intelligence Material, 11/13/62–11/30/62, John F. Kennedy Presidential Library, Boston, MA.

his revolution against the hegemon of the North, including with nuclear weapons, if necessary. This divergence demonstrated the degree to which Latin American regimes were out of step with their own publics. The governments of countries like Bolivia, Brazil, and Mexico, which had strong revolu-

Figure 13. Anti-U.S. protests even occurred in London, the capital of one of the firmest Western allies of the United States. (Don O'Brien/CC BY-SA 2.0)

tionary traditions and powerful domestic leftist movements, were unable to respond with the categorical condemnation of dictatorial regimes in the hemisphere. On the contrary, these states had to contend with opposition from the political right and left, with the more conservative sectors of society demanding a punitive response to Castro and the missile crisis, and the more progressive sectors of society adopting a pro-Castro stance. The missile crisis, therefore, had the effect of widening political divisions in many countries of the hemisphere.[361]

One positive outcome of the missile crisis was an enhanced awareness among key political actors in the hemisphere of the acute perils of nuclear brinkmanship. A mere month before the missile crisis erupted, the Brazilian delegation to the United Nations had submitted a draft resolution declaring Latin America a nuclear-free zone.[362] Though the proposal had been tabled, it was quickly resuscitated after news of the construction of the nuclear missile sites in Cuba broke. In November 1962, Brazil, Bolivia, Chile, and Ecuador introduced a draft resolution in the First Committee of the United Nations, and in April 1963, the presidents of these four countries, plus Mexican president López Mateos, issued a joint declaration of their intention to achieve the denuclearization of Latin America. These five countries were led by democratically elected presidents, who

361. Keller, "Latin American Missile Crisis," p. 198.

362. Bromley Smith, "Summary Record of NSC Executive Committee Meeting, October 26, 1962, 10:00 a.m.," in Chang and Kornbluh, eds., *Cuban Missile Crisis*, p. 180.

exercised foreign policies independent of the United States. Proposals to establish Latin America as a nuclear-free zone, though contentious, ultimately led to the 1967 signing of the Treaty for the Prohibition of Nuclear Weapons in Latin America, more popularly known as the Treaty of Tlatelolco, after the area of Mexico City where it was signed. Two years later, in 1969, the treaty entered into force after the requisite number of countries in the hemisphere ratified it. The ratifying countries pledged to keep all nuclear weapons out of their territory; to prohibit the development, testing, and importation of all such weapons; and to forbid the establishment of foreign nuclear bases.[363] In 1995, the last remaining holdout in the hemisphere—Cuba—signed the treaty.[364]

Conclusion: Lessons of the Cuban Missile Crisis

Perhaps the most fundamental lesson of the missile crisis was the alarming rapidity with which a localized conflict could escalate into nuclear war in the atomic age. Fears of nuclear annihilation not only led to the easing of tensions with the Soviet Union, culminating in the pursuit of détente under Richard Nixon and Henry Kissinger in the 1970s, but also seeped into U.S. popular culture. Director Stanley Kubrick's film *Dr. Strangelove or: How I Learned to Stop Worrying and Love the Bomb* was released in 1964 and satirically depicted the outbreak of nuclear war between the United States and the Soviet Union. The plot revolved around a deranged air force general—rumored to be based on Air Force chief of staff General Curtis LeMay—who orders a nuclear first strike against the Soviet Union. Nominated for four Academy Awards, the dark comedy was a box-office smash, and is still widely considered by film critics as one of the best political satires of the twentieth century.[365]

While fears of nuclear destruction led to the relaxation of tensions with the Soviet Union, however, the Kennedy administration did not alter its fundamental approach to Castro's Cuba. The administration pursued a

---

363. John R. Redick, "The Tlatelolco Regime and Nonproliferation in Latin America," *International Organization*, Vol. 35, No. 1 (Winter, 1981), pp. 106 and 110.

364. "Cuba Signs Treaty of Tlatelolco," *Arms Control Today*, Vol. 25, No. 3 (April 1995), p. 23.

365. For more, see Margot A. Henriksen, *Dr. Strangelove's America: Society and Culture in the Atomic Age* (Berkeley: University of California Press, 1997).

variety of measures to prevent communism from spreading further into Latin America. The Alliance for Progress was an extensive economic aid program that had been announced at the Punta del Este conference of the Organization of American States in 1961. It was explicitly envisioned as a means of helping Latin American countries develop their economies and thereby reduce opportunities for Soviet-Cuban communism to win the hearts and minds of the region's peasants and workers. By the time of the Cuban Missile Crisis—approximately a year after the Alliance for Progress was announced—U.S. policymakers recognized the myriad obstacles to its success. The bureaucratic channels through which aid to Latin America flowed were tied up with red tape, and the social goals of the aid frequently created political instability, especially in countries still governed by undemocratic regimes. Though there were a few success stories, ultimately, in the words of one prominent historian of U.S.-Latin American relations, "perhaps the best that could be said about the Alliance was that the infusion of money helped Latin America postpone the economic and financial disasters that hit the region in the 1980s."[366]

The Alliance for Progress, however, did not supersede the other main track of the Kennedy administration's policy toward Latin America: counterinsurgency efforts to crush the communist-inspired armed guerrilla movements that plagued nearly every country of the hemisphere. Massive infusions of military aid were designed to strengthen the counterinsurgency capabilities of the region's armed forces in the struggle against violent communism.[367] The source of ideological inspiration, training, and weapons for many of these guerrilla groups was, of course, Cuba. Thus, the Kennedy administration continued its feverish efforts to remove Castro from power, even after those efforts had contributed to the crisis that brought the world to the brink of nuclear annihilation. It was not until Kennedy's assassination in November 1963 that his successor, Lyndon Baines Johnson, discovered the extent of these efforts and altered U.S. policy toward Cuba, which would thereafter be characterized more by diplomatic and economic pressure than by a concerted campaign to either oust or kill Castro. Castro himself watched several subsequent U.S. presidents come and go, while he remained firmly in control of Cuba until his death in November 2016.

---

366. Rabe, *The Most Dangerous Area in the World*, p. 172.

367. Ibid., pp. 128–129.

For the Department of Defense, one of the most important lessons of the crisis was the significance of sea power. In a review of the crisis, DOD officials applauded the "ease with which the US was able to apply its will on the high seas," and asserted that Cuba was "a hostage to the US Navy." On balance, according to the Defense Department, "our power at sea, visibly capable of destroying enemy sea forces but used instead to apply political-military pressures, permitted us to retain the initiative and to succeed."[368] The skill and professionalism of U.S. naval forces helped prevent the quarantine from escalating into all-out war.

Another important lesson that Defense Department officials drew regarded the deterrent ability of nuclear weapons. Despite the fact that local U.S. nuclear superiority had not deterred the Soviets from providing Cuba with offensive nuclear weaponry, overall U.S. nuclear strength had constrained Moscow's ability to escalate. Moreover, Khrushchev's decision to supply Castro with the weapons in the first place had been premised on a view of Kennedy as weak and indecisive: "At the outset, the Soviets clearly lacked conviction that the US was determined to use force on this issue." Once the Kennedy administration implemented the naval quarantine, the Soviets were faced "with an impossible military problem locally."[369] Although Kennedy's waffling during the Bay of Pigs invasion in April 1961 had contributed to Khrushchev's impression of the U.S. president as a weak-willed naïf who could be easily pushed around, his determination to resolve the missile crisis peacefully while insisting upon the complete withdrawal of all Soviet-supplied offensive weaponry from Cuban territory did much to revive his reputation as a shrewd and sagacious statesman.

Fidel Castro, of course, outlived both Kennedy and Khrushchev. The U.S. president was assassinated in November 1963 by a deranged former Marine with documented sympathies for the Soviet Union and revolutionary Cuba. The assassination is still shrouded in mystery, serving to animate a variety of conspiracy theories. Lee Harvey Oswald's

---

368. Defense Department Review, "Some Lessons from Cuba," November 15, 1962, in Chang and Kornbluh, eds., *Cuban Missile Crisis*, pp. 317–318.

369. Defense Draft, Some Lessons from Cuba, February 14, 1963, National Security File, Country File, Cuba, Box 37A, Folder: Cuba, General, 2/63, John F. Kennedy Presidential Library, Boston, MA.

connections to Moscow and Havana are one such mystery. Because crucial information pertaining to these connections was suppressed or destroyed at the highest levels of the U.S. government, it is unlikely that these conspiracy theories will ever be completely dispelled.[370] As for the Soviet premier, he was abruptly thrown out of office in 1964, at least partly due to his disastrous handling of the missile crisis. Castro would never again trust the Soviets the way he did before the fiasco, and although he remained firmly in the Soviet communist camp, he focused on strengthening relations with independent-leaning states of the Western Hemisphere and with the countries of the Third World and the Non-Aligned Movement. He brought Cuba as a signatory to the Treaty of Tlatelolco in 1995, solidifying his commitment to denuclearizing Latin America and thereby ensuring that nothing like what happened during those thirteen dark and deadly days in October would ever transpire again.

Historiography of the Cuban Missile Crisis

The first wave of memoirs from members of the Kennedy administration shaped the early narrative of the missile crisis.[371] The most influential of these was undoubtedly Robert F. Kennedy's *Thirteen Days: A Memoir of the Cuban Missile Crisis*.[372] In it, Kennedy makes a number of claims that have since been shown to be false, based on documentary evidence in both written and audio form. Sheldon M. Stern of the John F. Kennedy Presidential Library in Boston was the first historian to examine the White House tape recordings made during the missile crisis. He

---

370. For more, see Jefferson Morley, *Our Man in Mexico: Winston Scott and the Hidden History of the CIA* (Lawrence: University Press of Kansas, 2008), pp. 183, 198–199, 208–211, and 224.

371. Among these influential memoirs can be counted Roger N. Hilsman, *To Move a Nation: The Politics of Foreign Policy in the Administration of John F. Kennedy* (New York: Doubleday, 1967); Arthur M. Schlesinger Jr., *A Thousand Days: John F. Kennedy in the White House* (Boston, MA: Houghton Mifflin, 1965); and Theodore C. Sorensen, *Kennedy* (New York: Harper and Row, 1965).

372. Robert F. Kennedy, *Thirteen Days: A Memoir of the Cuban Missile Crisis* (New York: W. W. Norton, 1969).

has demonstrated that Robert Kennedy's self-portrayal, as one of the more dovish members of the Executive Committee, was self-serving and incongruent with the facts.[373]

One defining characteristic of this first wave of scholarship is its singular focus on U.S. decision-making. The crisis is viewed as a classic Cold War confrontation between the United States and the Soviet Union, with Cuba serving as merely the origin and locale of events. Thus, very little attention was devoted to the fears, goals, and actions of the Cuban leadership, or the course of developments in relations between Moscow and Havana. In 1971, political scientists Graham Allison and Philip Zelikow published their seminal volume on the crisis, *Essence of Decision*.[374] The book was very much in line with the first wave of scholarship, placing U.S. decision-making at the forefront of their analysis. The work is also notable for the emphasis placed on Berlin in the strategic calculations of both the Americans and the Soviets.

The second wave of scholarship on the missile crisis emerged in the late 1980s, when a series of international conferences on the missile crisis revealed new evidence on Soviet perspectives. A number of works appeared that added the crucial but heretofore missing dimension of Soviet decision-making, not only in relation to the United States, but also in relation to Cuba as well. Perhaps the most important secondary source that is based upon Soviet archival evidence is Aleksandr Fursenko and Timothy Naftali's work *One Hell of a Gamble*.[375] Anastas Mikoyan's son, Sergo, has contributed a work that is part memoir, part history, aptly titled *The Soviet Cuban Missile Crisis*.[376]

373. Sheldon M. Stern, *The Cuban Missile Crisis in American Memory: Myths versus Reality* (Stanford, CA: Stanford University Press, 2012).

374. Graham Allison and Philip Zelikow, *Essence of Decision: Explaining the Cuban Missile Crisis, Second Edition* (New York: Longman, 1999).

375. Aleksandr Fursenko and Timothy Naftali, *One Hell of a Gamble: The Secret History of the Cuban Missile Crisis* (New York: W. W. Norton, 1997).

376. Sergo Mikoyan, *The Soviet Cuban Missile Crisis: Castro, Mikoyan, Kennedy, Khrushchev, and the Missiles of November* (Washington, DC: Woodrow Wilson Center Press, 2012).

Finally, a third wave of scholarship is currently focused on analyzing the regional and global implications of the crisis.[377] Some of these works focus on U.S. bilateral relations, while others examine regional and global politics and the ways in which they were upended by the missile crisis. The Cold War International History Project has been at the forefront of efforts to uncover new archival sources from the territories of the former Soviet Union, China, and from Latin American countries, above all, Cuba.[378] However, the lack of access to Cuban government archives continues to stymie scholars interested in uncovering Cuban perspectives on the crisis. Though the Cuban Missile Crisis is by some accounts the most thoroughly analyzed episode in history, there is still much work to be done.

---

377. For instance, James G. Hershberg, "The United States, Brazil, and the Cuban Missile Crisis, 1962," pts. 1 and 2, *Journal of Cold War Studies* Vol. 6, No. 2 (Spring 2004), pp. 3–20, and Vol. 6, No. 3 (Summer 2004), pp. 5–67; and Renata Keller, "The Latin American Missile Crisis," *Diplomatic History* Vol. 39, No. 2 (April 2015), pp. 195–222.

378. For instance, Cold War International History Project Bulletin, Issue 17/18, Fall 2012, *The Global Cuban Missile Crisis at 50: New Evidence From Behind the Iron, Bamboo, and Sugarcane Curtains and Beyond*, edited by James G. Hershberg and Christian F. Ostermann.

DOCUMENTS

DOCUMENT 1

Memorandum for McGeorge Bundy from Arthur Schlesinger Jr., April 10, 1961[1]

In this memorandum, penned a mere week before the launch of Brigade 2506, Arthur Schlesinger Jr., special aide to U.S. president John F. Kennedy, warns of the potential consequences of the Bay of Pigs invasion. He observes that many people do not view Cuba as a national security threat to the United States, and cautions that international public opinion will refuse to countenance "calculated aggression against a small nation in defiance both of treaty obligations and of the international standards we have repeatedly asserted against the Communist world." Schlesinger's predictions proved prescient; in this memo he anticipates almost exactly what the reaction would be after evidence of U.S. involvement in the invasion of Cuba surfaced.

A great many people simply do not at this moment see that Cuba presents so grave and compelling a threat to our national security as to justify a course of action which much of the world will interpret as calculated aggression against a small nation in defiance both of treaty obligations and of the international standards we have repeatedly asserted against the Communist world. . . . To say that the Russians are doing worse in Laos is true but irrelevant, since we profess to be acting according to higher motives and higher principles than the Russians. Because the

---

1. "Memorandum for McGeorge Bundy from Arthur Schlesinger Jr.," April 10, 1961, National Security File, Country File, Cuba, Box 35A, Folder: Cuba, General, 1/61/–4/61, John F. Kennedy Presidential Library, pp. 2–4, emphasis in the original.

alleged threat to our national security will not seem to many people great enough to justify so flagrant a violation of our professed principles, these people will assume that our action is provoked by a threat to something other than our security. Given the mythology of our relationship to Latin America, they will assume that we are acting, not to protect our safety, but to protect our property and investments. In short, for many people the easiest explanation of our action will be as a reversion to economic imperialism of the pre-World War I, Platt Amendment, big-stick, gunboat-diplomacy kind. . . . The Communists will next seek to use the alleged U.S. initiative to bolster the Marxist interpretation of history. They will portray it as an effort on the part of the greatest capitalist nation to punish a small country for its desire to achieve political and economic independence. Throughout the underdeveloped world, they will try to persuade local nationalists to identify Castro's cause with their own struggles. There will be particular emphasis . . . on Castro as the defender of the colored races against white imperialism. . . . The underdeveloped countries will be urged in the United Nations to defend their own future freedom of action by defending Castro; we can expect to be placed on the defensive in the U.N. for some time and to be subjected to a series of harassing debates and resolutions. Ex-colonial nations everywhere will be called on to identify their own problems with those of Castro.

DOCUMENT 2

State Department White Paper, April 1961[2]

In this State Department White Paper, Latin American opinion of Fidel Castro's Cuba is analyzed. According to State Department officials, members of several of Latin America's moderate democratic political parties fretted about the military buildup in Cuba, which they claimed was "converting a brother country into an instrument of the cold war." This document suggests that

---

2. State Department White Paper (Department of State Publication 7171, Inter-American Series 66, Released April 1961), National Security File, Country File, Cuba, Box 35A, Folder: Cuba, General, White Paper, 5/61, JFK Presidential Library, pp. 18–19 and 22–23.

even before the missile crisis, some progressive reformists in Latin America were concerned about the regional impact of the Cuban Revolution. The White Paper also details the growing Soviet military presence in Cuba.

Meeting in Lima at the end of February 1961, representatives of APRA of Peru, Acción Democrática of Venezuela, and similar political groups in other Latin American republics summed up the situation when they said of Cuba that its "revolutionary process, justified in the beginning, has been deflected by its present agents, converting a brother country into an instrument of the cold war, separating it, with suicidal premeditation, from the community of interests of the Latin American people." . . .

Since the middle of 1960, more than 30,000 tons of arms with an estimated value of $50 million have poured from beyond the Iron Curtain into Cuba in an ever-rising flood. The 8-hour military parade through Habana and the military maneuvers in January 1961 displayed Soviet JS-2 51-ton tanks, Soviet SU-100 assault guns, Soviet T-34 35-ton tanks, Soviet 76 mm. field guns. Except for motorized equipment, the Cuban armed forces have been reequipped by the Soviet bloc and are now dependent on the bloc for the maintenance of their armed power. Soviet and Czech military advisers and technicians have accompanied the flow of arms. . . . As a consequence of Soviet military aid, Cuba has today, except for the United States, the largest ground forces in the hemisphere—at least ten times as large as the military forces maintained by previous Cuban Governments including that of Batista. Estimates of the size of the Cuban military establishment range from 250,000 to 400,000.

DOCUMENT 3

From the Cable on the Conversation between Gromyko and Kennedy, October 18, 1962[3]

This conversation between U.S. president Kennedy and Soviet foreign minister Andrei Gromyko occurred two days after the president had received photographic evidence of the construction of missile sites in Cuba. Gromyko defends the Soviet-Cuban alliance, strenuously denying that Castro presents a national security threat to the United States or any other country in the Western Hemisphere. He deceptively masks the purpose of the Soviet military buildup in Cuba, falsely claiming that all Soviet-supplied weaponry was strictly defensive in nature. Kennedy cautions Gromyko that the situation "is, perhaps, the most dangerous since the end of the Second World War."

[Gromyko] Now I would like to expound the Soviet government's position on the Cuban issue and the USSR's assessment of the US actions. The Soviet government is standing for peaceful coexistence of states with different social systems, against interference of one state into internal affairs of others, against intervention of the large states into affairs of small countries. Literally, that is the core of the Soviet Union's foreign policy. It is well known to you, Mr. President, the attitude of the Soviet government and personally of N. S. Khrushchev towards dangerous developments connected with the US administration position on the issue of Cuba. An unrestrained anti-Cuban campaign has been going on in the US for a long time and apparently there is a certain US administration policy behind it. Right now the US is making an attempt to blockade Cuban trade with other states. There is a talk about a possibility of actions of organized policy in this region under the US aegis. But all of it equals a way that can lead to grave consequences to a misfortune for the whole mankind and we are confident that such an outcome is not desired by any people, including the people of the US. The US administration

---

3. "From the Cable on the Conversation between Gromyko and Kennedy," October 18, 1962, History and Public Policy Program Digital Archive, Archive of Foreign Policy, Russian Federation (AVPRF); http://digitalarchive.wilsoncenter.org/document/114511.

for some reasons considers that the Cubans must solve their domestic affairs not at their own discretion, but at the discretion of the US. But on what grounds? Cuba belongs to the Cuban people, not to the US or any other state. And since it is so, then why the statements are made in the US calling for invasion to Cuba? What do the US need Cuba for? Who can in earnest believe that Cuba represents a threat to the US? If we speak about dimensions and resources of the two countries—the US and Cuba—then it's clear that they are a giant and a baby. The flagrant groundlessness of such charges against Cuba is obvious. Cuba does not represent, and can't represent any threat to the countries of Latin America. It's strange to think as if small Cuba can encroach on independence of either this or that country of Latin America. Cuban leaders and personally Fidel Castro have declared more than once in front of the whole world and in a most solemn manner that Cuba does not intend to impose their system, that they are firmly favoring the non-interference of states into internal affairs of each other. . . . As far as the aid of the Soviet Union to Cuba is concerned, the Soviet government has declared and I have been instructed to reaffirm it once more, our aid pursues exclusively the object of rendering Cuba assistance to its defensive capacity and development of its peaceful economy. Neither industry nor agriculture in Cuba, neither land-improvement works nor training of the Cuban personnel carried out by the Soviet specialists to teach them use some defensive kinds of armaments can represent a threat to anybody. If the case was somewhat different, the Soviet government would never be involved in such aid. . . .

[Kennedy] The actions of the Soviet Union create a very complicated situation and I don't know where the whole thing can bring us. The present situation is, perhaps, the most dangerous since the end of the Second World War. We, certainly, take on trust statements of the Soviet Union about the sort of armaments supplied by you to Cuba. As President I am trying to restrain those people in the US who are favoring an invasion of Cuba. . . . During the last four days the administration has received information from different sources reporting without any doubt that the Soviets had supplied Cuban government several defensive antiaircraft missiles with 25 miles radius of action similar to earlier models of our missile 'Nike'. At the same time the Soviets apparently are supplying different radars and other electronic equipment which is necessary for their use. We can also confirm the presence of several torpedo boats of Soviet fabrication earring along missiles "vessel to vessel" with 15 miles radius of action. The number of Soviet military specialists, who nowadays either are in Cuba or on their way over there (roughly 3500 persons), corresponds to the object of rendering help for the installation and training how to use those means. . . .

[Gromyko] There is no proof of the presence in Cuba of any regular combat forces from any country of the Soviet bloc neither proof of conceding Russia a military base (on the island) in violation of 1934 treaty on Guantanamo, nor presence of offensive missiles "ground-ground" type or any other offensive potential either in the hands of Cubans or under surveillance of the Soviets. If the situation were different, the most serious questions would arise. . . .

[Kennedy] In all my actions I proceed with due regard for statements of the Soviet Union that the armaments supplied to Cuba have an exclusively defensive character. . . .

[Gromyko] For my part I assured President once more that the policy of the Soviet Union always has been and stays directed at strengthening the peace and elimination of differences in the relations among all the countries, first of all in the relations between the USSR and the US, with whom the Soviet Union wants to live in peace and friendship.

DOCUMENT 4

Telegram from Soviet Foreign Minister Gromyko to the CC CPSU, October 20, 1962[4]

In this telegram, Soviet foreign minister Andrei Gromyko reports to the Central Committee of the Communist Party of the USSR about his conversation with U.S. secretary of state Dean Rusk. Rusk informs Gromyko that the United States will not militarily intervene in Cuba provided the weapons being emplaced there are strictly defensive and Castro ceases his attempts to export the Cuban Revolution. Gromkyo rebukes Rusk for his alarmist

4. "Telegram from Soviet Foreign Minister Gromyko to the CC CPSU," October 20, 1962, History and Public Policy Program Digital Archive, AVPRF, copy courtesy of NSA; translation by Mark H. Doctoroff, http://digitalarchive.wilsoncenter.org /document/111779.

interpretation of the Soviet military buildup in Cuba, claiming that U.S. military bases pose a more pressing threat to the Soviet Union than Soviet bases to the United States. Unlike Anatoly Dobrynin, Gromyko knew the true nature of Operation Anadyr, and was baldly lying to Rusk about the defensive character of the Soviet-supplied weaponry. The conversation also reveals the extent to which the divisive issues of the Second World War continued to plague U.S.-Soviet relations.

On October 18 a conversation with Rusk took place. Rusk, continuing my conversation with Kennedy, touched on the Cuba issue. He said that President Kennedy considers that issue very important, that it carries great significance for the USA, since it concerns the security of the Western hemisphere. As the President said, the USA has no intention of intervening with its own armed forces in Cuba. But the USA proceeds from the fact that everything that is happening in Cuba is of a defensive nature and will not turn Cuba into an attack platform against the USA and the countries of Latin America. Besides this, Rusk announced, the USA, in defining its position on the Cuban issue, as announced by the President in his conversation with us, proceeds also from the fact that Cuba will not undertake actions aimed at foisting its system and regime on the other countries of Latin America. The government of the USA places extremely high significance on these two conditions. It would be hoped that neither the first, nor the second, would take place.

As far as the domestic regime on Cuba is concerned, the USA decisively views it as a regime which contradicts the interests of security in the Western hemisphere. Having heard Rusk out, I said that the Cuban issue had been caused by the hostile policy of the USA towards Cuba. The USA for some reason believes that it must dictate to the Cubans the sort of domestic regime that should exist in Cuba, and the social structure under which the Cubans should live. But on what basis is the USA trying to appropriate for itself the right to dictate to the Cubans how to conduct their internal affairs? There is no such basis, and such a basis cannot be. Cuba belongs to the Cubans, not to Americans. Perhaps, I declared, Rusk can tell me, whither the principles of the UN Charter in American policy towards Cuba? They're not there. The actions of the USA are in flagrant contradiction with these principles. The USA is undertaking steps to cause hunger in Cuba. The actions which it is undertaking towards this end unmask the USA policy even more clearly. The Cubans, with ever more decisiveness, are speaking out and will continue to speak out in defense of their country and will strengthen its defenses. The Soviet Union is helping Cuba. It is trying to provide the Cubans with grain, and help to put its economy on a sound footing. This cannot present any danger to the USA. Soviet specialists are helping Cuban soldiers to master certain types of defensive weapons. This can't present any threat to the USA either. Overall, so far as the declaration that Cuba may present a threat to the security of the USA and countries of Latin America is concerned, such declarations are evidently intended for naive people. Even Americans themselves don't believe it.

Rusk said that he does not agree that Cuba cannot present a threat to the USA. Cuba without the Soviet Union, he declared, is one thing; a Cuba where "Soviet operators" run things is something different. The USA government and he, Rusk, are baselessly scaring the American people with "Soviet operators," I answered. The Soviet Union is providing assistance to Cuba in only a few areas, including whatever we can do to strengthen its defensive capability. The Cuban themselves are running everything on Cuba, and the USA knows that perfectly well. The situation has rapidly worsened, declared Rusk, since July of this year. Before July the situation caused no alarm. But from July, Soviet weapons have flowed into Cuba. So far it seems, according to U.S. Government data, that these are defensive weapons. But it is unclear how the situation will develop in the future. . . . I said that the Cubans should have come to conclusions about their own defense from the intervention on Cuba by the immigrant riff-raff organized by the Americans and financed by them. . . .

Rusk expansively spoke of the "community of interests" of the countries of the Western Hemisphere. Not mentioning the "Monroe Doctrine," he essentially tried to defend it, stressing the solidarity of the countries of the Western Hemisphere and the community of interests of their security. I said that in the policy of the USA and in Rusk's considerations regarding Cuba the countries somehow get lost, while the discussion is about the hemisphere. But in this hemisphere there are sovereign countries. Each one of them has a right to decide its own internal affairs upon consideration by its people. Cuba is one of these sovereign states. Besides that, I declared, if Rusk's reasoning and the entire conception which the USA government defends were to be applied to Europe and to Asia, then no doubt the conclusions which would flow from that would not please the USA. It comes out that the Americans consider themselves to have a right to be in a number of countries of Europe, Asia, and other regions of the world, if sometimes they don't even ask them about this, while certain others cannot even respond to an appeal for assistance in providing its own people with bread and strengthening its security in the face of a threat of intervention. With such a conception the Soviet Union cannot agree. It is hoped that the USA government too will more soberly approach the entire Cuban issue and will reject a hostile policy toward Cuba. . . .

Yes, declared Rusk, but nonetheless Cuba has violated the peace on the continent, nonetheless, beginning in July, the situation has taken a dangerous turn. The Soviet Union appeared in Cuba. A large quantity of Soviet weapons appeared in Cuba. All this has complicated the situation. No matter how often Rusk repeats, I declared, the assertion about some sort of turn of events in July, about the danger allegedly emanating from Cuba, in actuality, the situation remains simpler. The Cubans want Cuba to belong to them, and not to the USA. Maybe Rusk will reject the presence of the USA, the presence of American military bases and numerous military advisers in such countries like Turkey, Pakistan, Japan, not even speaking about such countries as England, Italy, and a number of other countries of Western Europe, and also Asia and Africa. It appears that the USA can have military bases in these countries, conclude with them military agreements, while the Soviet Union cannot even provide assistance in support of the Cuban economy and for the strengthening of the defense capability of Cuba. Rusk said that the Soviet Union is exaggerating the significance of American foreign military bases. . . . Rusk declared that—whether I believe him or not—that's something else, but he categorically asserts that besides the territory of the USA itself, American missiles and atomic weapons are in only three countries. Here I said: without a doubt, of course, England is among those countries? Yes, declared Rusk, England is one of them. He didn't name the others. As far as Japan is concerned, declared Rusk, I categorically assert that neither missiles, nor nuclear weapons of the USA are in Japan. They don't have any of those weapons in South Korea either, if, of course, the actions of North Korea will not make it necessary to change that situation. . . .

He then began to speak on the subject of the policy of the Soviet Union after the Second World War, partly trying to tie these musings with the Cuban issue and partly with the issue of American foreign military bases. He said that "in the Stalinist period" the Soviet Union conducted a foreign policy which forced the USA to create its bases overseas and to deploy its forces there. He gave an alleged example—Korea and the Korean peninsula. He said, that before the events in Korea the USA in fact did not have a single division up to strength. At that time the USA practically did not have a battle-worthy army available. But the situation changed because of the Korean War. Before this there was such a thing as the Berlin Blockade, which also played a definite role in the change in the American policy. All this is reflected, said Rusk, in the armament program. He again began to speak about the influence of the "Stalinist policy" on the policy and actions of the Western powers. The Western powers, including the USA, cannot but take that into account even now. Responding to these statements of Rusk, I stressed that the Secretary of State of the USA had drawn an extremely depressing and one-sided picture of the foreign policy of the USSR in the postwar period, including during the Stalin period. No doubt Rusk, like other U.S. officials, will not deny a great historical fact: besides the fact that the army of the Soviet Union routed the Nazi army and as a powerful avalanche moved into Western Europe, it was not used contrary to the alliance agreements and had stopped following the defeat of Hitler's Germany. And in that situation, if the Soviet Union, the Soviet government, had had expansionist intentions, it could have occupied all of Western Europe. But the Soviet Union had not done that and had not started to do it. That already by itself is an eloquent answer to the attempt to cast doubt on the foreign policy of the Soviet Union and on its actions in the postwar period. You know, I declared to Rusk, that our CC and the Soviet government, at the initiative of N.S. Khrushchev, have taken a number of foreign policy steps which earlier had not been taken. You are familiar, no doubt, with that which has been done in the foreign policy of the USSR regarding the condemnation of Stalin's Cult of Personality. You know, in particular, about the signing of the Austrian State Treaty, which was evaluated positively throughout the world and which helped to make possible an improvement of the situation in central Europe. But we categorically reject any attempts to generalize or to draw conclusions about Soviet foreign policy in the postwar period, which USA government officials make with the intent, apparently, of whitewashing its own policy, in this case towards Cuba. . . . However, he at this point started to talk about the fact that the USA, at the end of the war, and also in the first postwar period to the greatest extent conducted itself well. It, declared Rusk, had not tried to use the advantage which it had at that time vis-à-vis its monopoly possession of the atomic bomb. I let him know that that, apparently, had not been so much because the United States had wanted to conduct itself well, as that the atomic bomb at that time could not play a decisive role in the serious standoff of the leading powers. Rusk did not challenge this declaration, but all the same expressed the thought that the USA had had an advantage at that time in its possession of the atomic bomb and that it had not even tried to use it politically. . . .

A short general evaluation of this conversation with Rusk: Rusk tried again to stress, obviously at Kennedy's behest, that the USA gives great importance to the Cuban issue and considers it the most painful for the USA. He only in passing touched on Kennedy's declaration, made in the conversation with us, about the fact that the USA has no intentions to intervene in Cuba (with a reservation regarding the threat to the security of the USA and the countries of Latin America). Rusk's reasoning revolved mostly around a circle of questions related to Soviet assistance to Cuba, primarily arms. By Rusk's behavior it was possible to observe how painfully the American leaders are suffering the fact that the Soviet Union decisively has stood on the side of Cuba, and that the Cubans are conducting themselves bravely and confidently. Kennedy managed to hide his feelings better. But he too, when he spoke about Cuba, formulated his ideas with emphasis, slowly, obviously weighing every word. It is characteristic that Rusk, during our entire conversation with Kennedy, sat absolutely silently, and red "like a crab." In the conversation with him later he couldn't hide his feelings very well.

DOCUMENT 5

President John F. Kennedy's Speech to the Nation, October 22, 1962[5]

In President Kennedy's speech to the nation, he reveals the extent and purpose of the Soviet military buildup in Cuba—to "provide a nuclear strike capability against the Western Hemisphere." He describes the strategic implications of the Soviet-supplied weapons systems, and lays out the U.S. response—to demand their immediate dismantlement and withdrawal, and to establish a

---

5. Available at https://sourcebooks.fordham.edu/mod/1962kennedy-cuba.html.

naval quarantine on all offensive military shipments to Cuba. Kennedy also calls for emergency sessions of the Organization of American States and the U.N. Security Council, and expresses his support for the Cuban people.

Good evening, my fellow citizens. This Government, as promised, has maintained the closest surveillance of the Soviet military build-up on the island of Cuba. Within the past week unmistakable evidence has established the fact that a series of offensive missile sites is now in preparation on that imprisoned island. The purposes of these bases can be none other than to provide a nuclear strike capability against the Western Hemisphere.

Upon receiving the first preliminary hard information of this nature last Tuesday morning (October 16) at 9:00 A.M., I directed that our surveillance be stepped up. And having now confirmed and completed our evaluation of the evidence and our decision on a course of action, this Government feels obliged to report this new crisis to you in fullest detail.

The characteristics of these new missile sites indicate two distinct types of installations. Several of them include medium-range ballistic missiles capable of carrying a nuclear warhead for a distance of more than 1,000 nautical miles. Each of these missiles, in short, is capable of striking Washington, D.C., the Panama Canal, Cape Canaveral, Mexico City, or any other city in the southeastern part of the United States, in Central America, or in the Caribbean area.

Additional sites not yet completed appear to be designed for intermediate-range ballistic missiles capable of traveling more than twice as far-and thus capable of striking most of the major cities in the Western Hemisphere, ranging as far north as Hudson Bay, Canada, and as far south as Lima, Peru. In addition, jet bombers, capable of carrying nuclear weapons, are now being uncrated and assembled in Cuba, while the necessary air bases are being prepared.

This urgent transformation of Cuba into an important strategic base— by the presence of these large, long-range, and clearly offensive weapons of sudden mass destruction—constitutes an explicit threat to the peace and security of all the Americas, in flagrant and deliberate defiance of the Rio Pact of 1947, the traditions of this nation and Hemisphere, the joint Resolution of the 87th Congress, the Charter of the United Nations, and my own public warnings to the Soviets on September 4 and 13.

This action also contradicts the repeated assurances of Soviet spokesmen, both publicly and privately delivered, that the arms build-up in Cuba would retain its original defensive character and that the Soviet Union had no need or desire to station strategic missiles on the territory of any other nation.

The size of this undertaking makes clear that it has been planned for some months. Yet only last month, after I had made clear the distinction between any introduction of ground-to-ground missiles and the existence of defensive antiaircraft missiles, the Soviet Government publicly stated on September 11 that, and I quote, "The armaments and military equipment sent to Cuba are designed exclusively for defensive purposes," and, and I quote the Soviet Government, "There is no need for the Soviet Government to shift its weapons for a retaliatory blow to any other country, for instance Cuba," and that, and I quote the Government, "The Soviet Union has so powerful rockets to carry these nuclear warheads that there is no need to search for sites for them beyond the boundaries of the Soviet Union." That statement was false.

Only last Thursday, as evidence of this rapid offensive build-up was already in my hand, Soviet Foreign Minister Gromyko told me in my office that he was instructed to make it clear once again, as he said his Government had already done, that Soviet assistance to Cuba, and I quote, "pursued solely the purpose of contributing to the defense capabilities of Cuba," that, and I quote him, "training by Soviet specialists of Cuban nationals in handling defensive armaments was by no means offensive," and that "if it were otherwise," Mr. Gromyko went on, "the Soviet Government would never become involved in rendering such assistance." That statement also was false.

Neither the United States of America nor the world community of nations can tolerate deliberate deception and offensive threats on the part of any nation, large or small. We no longer live in a world where only the actual firing of weapons represents a sufficient challenge to a nation's security to constitute maximum peril. Nuclear weapons are so destructive and ballistic missiles are so swift that any substantially increased possibility of their use or any sudden change in their deployment may well be regarded as a definite threat to peace.

For many years both the Soviet Union and the United States, recognizing this fact, have deployed strategic nuclear weapons with great care, never upsetting the precarious status quo which insured that these weapons would not be used in the absence of some vital challenge. Our own strategic missiles have never been transferred to the territory of any other nation under a cloak of secrecy and deception; and our history, unlike that of the Soviets since the end of World War II, demonstrates that we have no desire to dominate or conquer any other nation or impose our system upon its people. Nevertheless, American citizens have become adjusted to living daily on the bull's eye of Soviet missiles located inside the U.S.S.R. or in submarines.

In that sense missiles in Cuba add to an already clear and present danger—although it should be noted the nations of Latin America have never previously been subjected to a potential nuclear threat.

But this secret, swift, and extraordinary build-up of Communist missiles—in an area well known to have a special and historical relationship to the United States and the nations of the Western Hemisphere, in violation of Soviet assurances, and in defiance of American and hemispheric policy—this sudden, clandestine decision to station strategic weapons for the first time outside of Soviet soil—is a deliberately provocative and unjustified change in the status quo which cannot be accepted by this country if our courage and our commitments are ever to be trusted again by either friend or foe.

The 1930's taught us a clear lesson: Aggressive conduct, if allowed to grow unchecked and unchallenged, ultimately leads to war. This nation is opposed to war. We are also true to our word. Our unswerving objective, therefore, must be to prevent the use of these missiles against this or any other country and to secure their withdrawal or elimination from the Western Hemisphere.

Our policy has been one of patience and restraint, as befits a peaceful and powerful nation, which leads a world-wide alliance. We have been determined not to be diverted from our central concerns by mere irritants and fanatics. But now further action is required—and it is underway; and these actions may only be the beginning. We will not prematurely or unnecessarily risk the costs of worldwide nuclear war in which even the fruits of victory would be ashes in our mouth—but neither will we shrink from that risk at any time it must be faced.

Acting, therefore, in the defense of our own security and of the entire Western Hemisphere, and under the authority entrusted to me by the Constitution as endorsed by the resolution of the Congress, I have directed that the following initial steps be taken immediately:

First: To halt this offensive build-up, a strict quarantine on all offensive military equipment under shipment to Cuba is being initiated. All ships of any kind bound for Cuba from whatever nation or port will, if found to contain cargoes of offensive weapons, be turned back: This quarantine will be extended, if needed, to other types of cargo and carriers. We are not at this time, however, denying the necessities of life as the Soviets attempted to do in their Berlin blockade of 1948.

Second: I have directed the continued and increased close surveillance of Cuba and its military build-up. The Foreign Ministers of the Organization of American States in their communiqué of October 3 rejected secrecy on such matters in this Hemisphere. Should these offensive military preparations continue, thus increasing the threat to the Hemisphere, further action will be justified. I have directed the Armed Forces to prepare for any eventualities; and I trust that in the interests of both the Cuban people and the Soviet technicians at the sites, the hazards to all concerned of continuing this threat will be recognized.

Third: It shall be the policy of this nation to regard any nuclear missile launched from Cuba against any nation in the Western Hemisphere as an attack by the Soviet Union on the United States, requiring a full retaliatory response upon the Soviet Union.

Fourth: As a necessary military precaution I have reinforced our base at Guantanamo, evacuated today the dependents of our personnel there, and ordered additional military units to be on a standby alert basis.

Fifth: We are calling tonight for an immediate meeting of the Organ of Consultation, under the Organization of American States, to consider this threat to hemispheric security and to invoke articles six and eight of the Rio Treaty in support of all necessary action. The United Nations Charter allows for regional security arrangements—and the nations of this Hemisphere decided long ago against the military presence of outside powers. Our other allies around the world have also been alerted.

Sixth: Under the Charter of the United Nations, we are asking tonight that an emergency meeting of the Security Council be convoked without delay to take action against this latest Soviet threat to world peace. Our resolution will call for the prompt dismantling and withdrawal of all offensive weapons in Cuba, under the supervision of United Nations observers, before the quarantine can be lifted.

Seventh and finally: I call upon Chairman Khrushchev to halt and eliminate this clandestine, reckless, and provocative threat to world peace and to stable relations between our two nations. I call upon him further to abandon this course of world domination and to join in an historic effort to end the perilous arms race and transform the history of man. He has an opportunity now to move the world back from the abyss of destruction—by returning to his Government's own words that it had no need to station missiles outside its own territory, and withdrawing these weapons from Cuba—by refraining from any action which will widen or deepen the present crisis—and then by participating in a search for peaceful and permanent solutions.

This nation is prepared to present its case against the Soviet threat to peace, and our own proposals for a peaceful world, at any time and in any forum in the Organization of American States, in the United Nations, or in any other meeting that could be useful—without limiting our freedom of action.

We have in the past made strenuous efforts to limit the spread of nuclear weapons. We have proposed the elimination of all arms and military bases in a fair and effective disarmament treaty. We are prepared to discuss new proposals for the removal of tensions on both sides—including the possibilities of a genuinely independent Cuba, free to determine its own destiny. We have no wish to war with the Soviet Union, for we are a peaceful people who desire to live in peace with all other peoples.

But it is difficult to settle or even discuss these problems in an atmosphere of intimidation. That is why this latest Soviet threat—or any other threat which is made either independently or in response to our actions this week—must and will be met with determination. Any hostile move anywhere in the world against the safety and freedom of peoples to whom we are committed—including in particular the brave people of West Berlin—will be met by whatever action is needed.

Finally, I want to say a few words to the captive people of Cuba, to whom this speech is being directly carried by special radio facilities. I speak to you as a friend, as one who knows of your deep attachment to your fatherland, as one who shares your aspirations for liberty and justice for all. And I have watched and the American people have watched with deep sorrow how your nationalist revolution was betrayed and how your fatherland fell under foreign domination. Now your leaders are no longer Cuban leaders inspired by Cuban ideals. They are puppets and agents of an international conspiracy which has turned Cuba against your friends and neighbors in the Americas—and turned it into the first

Latin American country to become a target for nuclear war, the first Latin American country to have these weapons on its soil.

These new weapons are not in your interest. They contribute nothing to your peace and well-being. They can only undermine it. But this country has no wish to cause you to suffer or to impose any system upon you. We know that your lives and land are being used as pawns by those who deny you freedom.

Many times in the past Cuban people have risen to throw out tyrants who destroyed their liberty. And I have no doubt that most Cubans today look forward to the time when they will be truly free—free from foreign domination, free to choose their own leaders, free to select their own system, free to own their own land, free to speak and write and worship without fear or degradation. And then shall Cuba be welcomed back to the society of free nations and to the associations of this Hemisphere.

My fellow citizens, let no one doubt that this is a difficult and dangerous effort on which we have set out. No one can foresee precisely what course it will take or what costs or casualties will be incurred. Many months of sacrifice and self-discipline lie ahead—months in which both our patience and our will will be tested, months in which many threats and denunciations will keep us aware of our dangers. But the greatest danger of all would be to do nothing.

The path we have chosen for the present is full of hazards, as all paths are; but it is the one most consistent with our character and courage as a nation and our commitments around the world. The cost of freedom is always high—but Americans have always paid it. And one path we shall never choose, and that is the path of surrender or submission.

Our goal is not the victory of might but the vindication of right—not peace at the expense of freedom, but both peace and freedom, here in this Hemisphere and, we hope, around the world. God willing, that goal will be achieved.

DOCUMENT 6

Resolution Adopted by the Council of the Organization of American States Acting Provisionally as the Organ of Consultation, October 23, 1962[6]

The Council of the Organization of American States determines that the presence of nuclear missiles in Cuba threatens the entire hemisphere and calls for the immediate dismantlement and withdrawal of all offensive weapons from Cuban territory. The council also recommends that all member states of the OAS "take all measures . . . including the use of armed force" if necessary to prevent the Cuban government from continuing to receive weaponry from the communist bloc. Finally, the council hopes that the U.N. Security Council will dispatch observers to Cuba—a measure that Castro fiercely resisted.

Incontrovertible evidence has appeared that the Government of Cuba, despite repeated warnings, has secretly endangered the peace of the Continent by permitting the Sino-Soviet powers to have intermediate and middle-range missiles on its territory capable of carrying nuclear warheads; The Council of the Organization of American States, meeting as the Provisional Organ of Consultation, Resolves: 1. To call for the immediate dismantling and withdrawal from Cuba of all missiles and other weapons with any offensive capability; 2. To recommend that the member states, in accordance with Articles 6 and 8 of the Inter-American Treaty of Reciprocal Assistance, take all measures, individually and collectively including the use of armed force, which they may deem necessary to ensure that the Government of Cuba cannot continue to receive from the Sino-Soviet powers military material and related supplied which may threaten the peace and security of the Continent and to prevent the missiles in Cuba with offensive capability from ever becoming an active threat to the peace and security of the Continent; 3. To inform the

---

6. "Resolution Adopted by the Council of the Organization of American States Acting Provisionally as the Organ of Consultation," October 23, 1962, National Security File, Country File, Cuba, Box 54, Folder: Cuba, Subjects, OAS 1961–1962, JFK Presidential Library.

Security Council of the United Nations of this resolution in accordance with Article 54 of the Charter of the United Nations and to express the hope that the Security Council will, in accordance with the draft resolution introduced by the United States, dispatch United Nations observers to Cuba at the earliest moment.

DOCUMENT 7

Message from Mexican President Adolfo López Mateos to Cuban President Osvaldo Dorticós, October 23, 1962[7]

In this message to Cuban president Osvaldo Dorticós, Mexican president Adolfo López Mateos expresses his concern that the presence of offensive weaponry poses a security threat to the entire hemisphere. Mateos urges Dorticós to withdraw the missiles and to not allow Cuban territory to be used as a Soviet military base. This document is noteworthy because Mexico was one of the biggest Latin American supporters of the Cuban Revolution.

Mr. President:

On board [a] plane on [a] return flight to my country ['patria'] after a friendly mission to four countries in Asia, the essence of which was to express the need to preserve peace, to seek an end to the arms race, and to abolish the manufacture and use of nuclear weapons, I learned of President Kennedy's message, in which he reported on the installation in Cuba of platforms to launch missiles of medium and long range capacity able to transport nuclear weapons. In repeated occasions, your

---

7. "Message from Mexican President Adolfo López Mateos to Cuban President Osvaldo Dorticós," October 23, 1962, History and Public Policy Program Digital Archive, Archivo Histórico Diplomático Genaro Estrada, Secretaría de Relaciones Exteriores, Mexico City. Obtained by James Hershberg, translated by Eduardo Baudet and Tanya Harmer, http://digitalarchive.wilsoncenter.org/document/115225.

ambassadors in Mexico Mr. [Jose Antonio] Portuondo and [Carlos] Lechuga [soon to become Cuban ambassador to the United Nations] assured me that the Cuban government was only receiving defensive weaponry and training for its use but that there was no intention at all of acquiring or installing any type of aggressive weapons and even less so of so-called atomic [bombs]. I consider that the possible existence of the installations of the type referred to could constitute a serious threat not only to the security of the peoples in the American continent but for the peace of the world. I think that neither the government nor the Cuban people wish to be constituted as a threat to the peoples of America nor as factors that may lead to a breach of the peace. Humanity as a whole would be in danger. In the name of the friendly relations that unite and have united our countries, I fervently wish that Cuban territory has not become a base for weapons of aggression and in the case that this were to have occurred, I believe it is my duty in the name of peace which all the Mexicans have the wish to preserve, to cordially make a call to your government so that those bases are not used in any form whatsoever and the offensive weapons are withdrawn from Cuban territory.

DOCUMENT 8

Letter from Khrushchev to John F. Kennedy, October 24, 1962[8]

In this letter to President Kennedy, noteworthy for its extravagant rhetoric, Soviet premier Nikita Khrushchev expresses outrage at the imposition of the U.S. naval quarantine and defends Soviet military support for Cuba. Khrushchev viewed Kennedy as weak and indecisive; this assessment of the president's character is reflected in the Soviet leader's belittling tone and withering criticism.

---

8. "Letter from Khrushchev to John F. Kennedy," October 24, 1962, History and Public Policy Program Digital Archive, Library of Congress, http://digitalarchive.wilsoncenter.org/document/111552.

Dear Mr. President,

...

Imagine, Mr. President, what if we were to present to you such an ultimatum as you have presented to us by your actions. How would you react to it? I think you would be outraged at such a move on our part. And this we would understand.

Having presented these conditions to us, Mr. President, you have thrown down the gauntlet. Who asked you to do this? By what right have you done this? Our ties with the Republic of Cuba, as well as our relations with other nations, regardless of their political system, concern only the two countries between which these relations exist. And, if it were a matter of quarantine as mentioned in your letter, then, as is customary in international practice, it can be established only by states agreeing between themselves, and not by some third party. Quarantines exist, for example, on agricultural goods and products. However, in this case we are not talking about quarantines, but rather about much more serious matters, and you yourself understand this.

... You, Mr. President, are not declaring a quarantine, but rather issuing an ultimatum, and you are threatening that if we do not obey your orders, you will then use force. Think about what you are saying! And you want to persuade me to agree to this! What does it mean to agree to these demands? It would mean for us to conduct our relations with other countries not by reason, but by yielding to tyranny. You are not appealing to reason; you want to intimidate us.

No, Mr. President, I cannot agree to this, and I think that deep inside, you will admit that I am right. I am convinced that if you were in my place you would do the same.

... This Organization [of American States] has no authority or grounds whatsoever to pass resolutions like those of which you speak in your letter. Therefore, we do not accept these resolutions. International law exists, generally accepted standards of conduct exist. We firmly adhere to the principles of international law and strictly observe the standards regulating navigation on the open sea, in international waters. We observe these standards and enjoy the rights recognized by all nations.

You want to force us to renounce the rights enjoyed by every sovereign state; you are attempting to legislate questions of international law; you are violating the generally accepted standards of this law. All this is due not only to hatred for the Cuban people and their government, but also for reasons having to do with the election campaign in the USA.

What morals, what laws can justify such an approach by the American government to international affairs? Such morals and laws are not to be found, because the actions of the USA in relation to Cuba are outright piracy. This, if you will, is the madness of a degenerating imperialism. Unfortunately, people of all nations, and not least the American people themselves, could suffer heavily from madness such as this, since with the appearance of modern types of weapons, the USA has completely lost its former inaccessibility.

Therefore, Mr. President, if you weigh the present situation with a cool head without giving way to passion, you will understand that the Soviet Union cannot afford not to decline the despotic demands of the USA. When you lay conditions such as these before us, try to put yourself in our situation and consider how the USA would react to such conditions. I have no doubt that if anyone attempted to dictate similar conditions to you—the USA, you would reject such an attempt. And we likewise say—no.

The Soviet government considers the violation of the freedom of navigation in international waters and air space to constitute an act of aggression propelling humankind into the abyss of a world nuclear-missile war. Therefore, the Soviet government cannot instruct captains of Soviet ships bound for Cuba to observe orders of American naval forces blockading this island. Our instructions to Soviet sailors are to observe strictly the generally accepted standards of navigation in international waters and not retreat one step from them. And, if the American side violates these rights, it must be aware of the responsibility it will bear for this act. To be sure, we will not remain mere observers of pirate actions by American ships in the open sea. We will then be forced on our part to take those measures we deem necessary and sufficient to defend our rights. To this end we have all that is necessary.

Respectfully, /s/ N. Khrushchev

DOCUMENT 9

Telegram from Soviet Ambassador to the USA Dobrynin to the USSR MFA, October 24, 1962[9]

In this telegram to the Soviet Foreign Ministry, Ambassador Dobrynin relays the content of his conversation with Robert Kennedy, the president's brother and attorney general. Kennedy castigates the Soviet ambassador for deceiving him about the true nature of the Soviet military buildup in Cuba. This document reveals the extent to which both Kennedys felt personally betrayed.

Late in the evening of October 23, R. Kennedy came to visit me. He was in an obviously excited condition and his speech was rich in repetitions and digressions. R. Kennedy said approximately the following.

I came on my own personal initiative without any assignment from the President. I considered it necessary to do this in order to clarify what exactly led to the current, extremely serious development of events. Most important is the fact that the personal relations between the President and the Soviet premier have suffered heavy damage. President Kennedy feels deceived and these feelings found their own reflection in his appeal to the American people.

From the very beginning, continued R. Kennedy, the Soviet side— N.S. Khrushchev, the Soviet government in its pronouncements and the Soviet ambassador during confidential meetings—have stressed the defensive nature of the weapons which are being delivered to Cuba. You, for instance, said R. Kennedy to me, told me about the exclusively defensive goals of the delivery of Soviet weapons, in particular, the missile weapons, during our meeting at the beginning of September. I understood you then as saying that we were talking only about /and in the future, too/ missiles of a relatively small range of action for the defense of Cuba itself and the approaches to it, but not about long-range missiles

---

9. "Telegram from Soviet Ambassador to the USA Dobrynin to the USSR MFA," October 24, 1962, History and Public Policy Program Digital Archive, AVPRF, copy courtesy of NSA; translation by Mark Doctoroff, http://digitalarchive.wilsoncenter.org /document/111625.

which could strike practically the entire territory of the USA. I told this to the President, who accepted it with satisfaction as the position of the Soviet government. There was a TASS declaration in the name of the Soviet government in which it was clearly stated that all military deliveries to Cuba are intended exclusively for defensive goals. The President and the government of the USA understood this as the true position of the USSR.

With even greater feelings of trust we took the corresponding declarations /public and confidential/ of the head of the Soviet government, who, despite the big disagreements and frequent aggravations in relations between our countries, the President has always trusted on a personal level. The message which had been sent by N.S. Khrushchev via the Soviet ambassador and [Kennedy adviser Theodore] Sorensen, about the fact that during the election campaign in the USA the Soviet side would not do anything to complicate the international situation and worsen relations between our countries, had made a great impression on the President.

All this led to the fact that the President believed everything which was said from the Soviet side, and in essence staked on that card his own political fate, having publicly announced to the USA, that the arms deliveries to Cuba carry a purely defensive character, although a number of Republicans have asserted to the contrary. And then the President suddenly receives trustworthy information to the effect that in Cuba, contrary to everything which had been said by the Soviet representatives, including the latest assurances, made very recently by A. A. Gromyko during his meeting with the President, there had appeared Soviet missiles with a range of action which cover almost the entire territory of the USA. Is this weapon really for the defensive purposes about which you, Mr. Ambassador, A. A. Gromyko, the Soviet government and N.S. Khrushchev had spoken?

The President felt himself deceived, and deceived intentionally. He is convinced of that even now. It was for him a great disappointment, or, speaking directly, a heavy blow to everything in which he had believed and which he had strived to preserve in personal relations with the head of the Soviet government: mutual trust in each other's personal assurances. As a result, the reaction which had found its reflection in the President's declaration and the extremely serious current events which are connected with it and which can still lead no one knows where.

Stressing with great determination that I reject his assertions about some sort of "deception" as entirely not corresponding to reality and as presenting the actions and motives of the Soviet side in a perverted light, I asked R. Kennedy why the President—if he had some sort of doubts—had not negotiated directly and openly with A. A. Gromyko, with whom there had been a meeting just a few days ago, but rather had begun actions, the seriousness of the consequences of which for the entire world are entirely unforeseeable. Before setting off on that dangerous path, fraught with a direct military confrontation between our countries, why not use, for instance, the confidential channels which we have and appeal directly to the head of the Soviet government.

R. Kennedy said the President had decided not to address A. A. Gromyko about this for the following two reasons: first, everything which the Soviet minister had set forth had, evidently according to the instructions of the Soviet government, been expressed in very harsh tones, so a discussion with him hardly could have been of much use; second, he had once again asserted the defensive character of the deliveries of Soviet weapons, although the President at that moment knew that this is not so, that they had deceived him again. As far as the confidential channel is concerned, what sense would that have made, if on the highest level—the level of the Minister of Foreign Affairs—precisely the same is said, although the facts are directly contradictory[?] To that same point, added R. Kennedy, long ago I myself in fact received the same sort of assurances from the Soviet ambassador, however, all that subsequently turned out to be entirely not so.

—Tell me,—R. Kennedy said to me further—[do] you, as the Soviet ambassador, have from your government information about the presence now in Cuba of around half a dozen (here he corrected himself, saying that that number may not be entirely accurate, but the fact remains a fact) missiles, capable of reaching almost any point in the United States?

In my turn I asked R. Kennedy why I should believe his information, when he himself does not want to recognize or respect that which the other side is saying to him. To that same point, even the President himself in his speech in fact had spoken only about some emplacements for missiles, which they allegedly had "observed," but not about the missiles themselves.

—There, you see—R. Kennedy quickly put forth,—what would have been the point of us contacting you via the confidential channel, if, as it appears, even the Ambassador, who has, as far as we know, the full trust of his government, does not know that long-range missiles which can strike the USA, rather than defensive missiles which are capable of defending Cuba from any sort of attack on the approaches to it, have already been provided to Cuba[?] It comes out that when you and I spoke earlier, you also did not have reliable information, although the conversation was about the defensive character of those weapons deliveries, including the future deliveries to Cuba, and everything about this was passed on to the President.

I categorically responded to R. Kennedy's thoughts about the information which I had received from the government, stressing that this was exclusively within the competence of the Soviet government. Simultaneously, his thoughts of "deception" were rejected again. Further, in calm but firm tones I set forth in detail our position on the Cuban issue, taking into account the Soviet government's latest announcement on Cuba, N.S. Khrushchev's letter in response to the President, and also other speeches and conversations of N.S. Khrushchev.

I particularly stressed the circumstance that, as far as is known to me, the head of the Soviet government values the warm relations with the President. N.S. Khrushchev recently spoke about that in particular in a conversation with [U.S.] Ambassador [to Moscow Foy] Kohler. I hope that the President also maintains the same point of view,—I added. On the relationships between the heads of our governments, on which history has placed special responsibility for the fate of the world, a lot really does depend; in particular, whether there will be peace or war. The Soviet government acts only in the interests of preserving and strengthening peace and calls on the United States government to act this way too. Stressing again the basic principles of our policy on which we will insist without any compromises (in the spirit of our declaration and N.S. Khrushchev's response letter), I simultaneously expressed the hope that the USA government show prudence and refrain from taking any actions which can lead to catastrophic consequences for peace in the whole world.

R. Kennedy, after repeating what he had already said about the President's moods (around this time he cooled down a bit and spoke in calmer tones), said that the President also values his relations with N.S. Khrushchev. As far as the future course of actions is concerned, then he, R. Kennedy, cannot add anything to that which had been said by the President himself, who stressed all the seriousness of the situation and understands with what sort of dangerous consequences all this may be connected, but he cannot act in any other way.

I once again set forth to him our position in the above-mentioned spirit.

Saying goodbye, already at the door of the Embassy, R. Kennedy as if by the way asked what sorts of orders the captains of the Soviet ships bound for Cuba have, in light of President Kennedy's speech yesterday and the declaration which he had just signed about the inadmissibility of bringing offensive weapons to Cuba.

I answered R. Kennedy with what I knew about the instructions which had been given earlier to the captains: not to obey any unlawful demands to stop or be searched on the open sea, as a violation of international norms of freedom of navigation. This order, as far as I know, has not been changed.

R. Kennedy, having waved his hand, said: I don't know how all this will end, for we intend to stop your ships. He left right after this.

Overall, his visit left a somewhat strange impression. He had not spoken about the future and paths toward a settlement of the conflict, making instead a "psychological" excursion, as if he was trying to justify the actions of his brother, the President, and put the responsibility for his hasty decision, in the correctness of which they and he, evidently, are not entirely confident, on us.

We think that in the interests of the affair it would be useful, using this opportunity to pass on to the President, through R. Kennedy, with whom I could meet again, in confidential form N.S. Khrushchev's thoughts on this matter, concerning not only the issues which R. Kennedy had touched on, but a wider circle of issues in light of the events which are going on now.

DOCUMENT 10

Memorandum for President Kennedy from Douglas Dillon, October 26, 1962[10]

In this memorandum to President Kennedy, Secretary of the Treasury C. Douglas Dillon argues that by providing nuclear

---

10. "Memorandum for President Kennedy from Douglas Dillon," October 26, 1962; National Security File, Country File, Cuba, Box 36A, Folder: Cuba, General, 10/26/62–10/27/62, JFK Presidential Library.

weapons to Cuba, the Soviets had thrown down the gauntlet and U.S. credibility was on the line. If the Kennedy administration failed to firmly counter Soviet actions, it risked losing the entire Latin American region to communism. This document reveals how important considerations of honor and prestige were in shaping the U.S. response to the crisis.

It is my view that the Soviet Union has now deliberately initiated a public test of our intentions that can determine the future course of world events for many years to come. If we allow the offensive capabilities presently in Cuba to remain there, I am convinced that sooner or later and probably sooner we will lose all Latin America to Communism because all credibility of our willingness to effectively resist Soviet military power will have been removed in the eyes of the Latins. . . . I believe that, in the interests of the survival of the entire free world fabric, we must be prepared to accept the public opinion results of a surprise strike, placing the full blame on Cuba for ignoring our clear and repeated warnings as well as the strong views of the other American states.

DOCUMENT 11

Telegram from Fidel Castro to N. S. Khrushchev, October 26, 1962[11]

In what has become known as his "Doomsday letter," Fidel Castro appears to advocate a nuclear strike against the United States, in the event of a direct invasion of Cuba. Though Castro later claimed he was not advocating a nuclear first strike, Khrushchev was sufficiently concerned by the contents of the letter to

---

11. "Telegram from Fidel Castro to N. S. Khrushchev," October 26, 1962, History and Public Policy Program Digital Archive, Archive of Foreign Policy, Russian Federation (AVPRF), http://digitalarchive.wilsoncenter.org/document/114501.

reevaluate whether Soviet offensive weaponry should ever be allowed in Cuban hands.

Dear Comrade KHRUSHCHEV,

In analyzing the situation that has arisen through the information at our disposal, it seems that aggression in the next 24 to 72 hours is almost inevitable.

Two variants of this aggression are possible:

1. The most likely one is an air attack on certain installations, with the aim of destroying those installations.

2. A less likely, but still possible variant is a direct invasion of the country. I believe that the realization of this variant would require large forces, and that this may hold the aggressors back; moreover such an aggression would be met with indignation by global public opinion.

You can be sure that we will offer strong and decisive resistance to whatever form this aggression may take.

The morale of the Cuban people is exceptionally high, and will face the aggression heroically.

Now I would like to express in a few words my deeply personal opinion on the events which are now occurring.

If an aggression of the second variant occurs, and the imperialists attack Cuba with the aim of occupying it, then the danger posed by such an aggressive measure will be so immense for all humanity that the Soviet Union will in circumstances be able to allow it, or to permit the creation of conditions in which the imperialists might initiate a nuclear strike against the USSR as well.

I say this because I believe that the aggressiveness of the imperialists is becoming extremely dangerous.

If they initiate an attack on Cuba—a barbaric, illegal, and amoral act—then in those circumstances the moment would be right for considering the elimination of such a danger, claiming the lawful right to self-defense. However difficult and horrifying this decision may be, there is, I believe, no other recourse. This opinion of mine has been formed by the emergence of an aggressive policy in which the imperialists ignore not only public opinion but all principles and rights as well: they blockade the sea, they violate air space, they are preparing an attack, and moreover they are destroying all possibilities for negotiations, even though they are aware of the gravity of the consequences.

You have been and remain a tireless defender of peace, and I understand how difficult these hours are for you, when the results of your superhuman efforts in the struggle for peace are so gravely threatened.

However, we will keep hoping up to the last minute that peace will be maintained, and we will do everything in our power to pursue this aim, but at the same time we are realistically evaluating the situation, and are ready and resolved to face any ordeal.

I once again express our whole country's endless gratitude to the Soviet people, who have shown such brotherly generosity towards us. We also express our admiration and deep thanks to you personally, and wish you success in your immense and crucial endeavor.

With brotherly greetings,
FIDEL CASTRO.

DOCUMENT 12

Letter from Khrushchev to Fidel Castro, October 28, 1962[12]

In his reply to Castro, Khrushchev lays out the terms for the withdrawal of the missiles. The Soviet premier urges Castro to show restraint, and attempts to convince him that Kennedy's pledge not to invade the island represents a victory for the socialist bloc and for the Cuban Revolution. Khrushchev's pleas for Castro to remain calm reveal his deep concern that the Cuban leader's impulsiveness could lead to open war with the United States.

Dear Comrade Fidel Castro:

Our message of 27 October to President Kennedy makes it possible to normalize the situation to our advantage, and to protect Cuba from invasion and war. Kennedy's response, which you appear familiar with,

---

12. "Letter from Khrushchev to Fidel Castro," October 28, 1962, History and Public Policy Program Digital Archive, Archive of Foreign Policy, Russian Federation (AVPRF), http://digitalarchive.wilsoncenter.org/document/114504.

provides a guarantee that the USA will refrain from invading Cuba not only with its own forces, but with those of its allies as well; the President of the USA responds with agreement to my messages of 26 and 27 October 1962.

We have now composed our response to the President's response message. I will not give you a lengthy account of it, since you will become familiar with the text that is being broadcast now by radio.

In connection with this we would like to recommend to you now, at this critical moment, not to yield to your emotions, to show restraint. It must be said that we understand your indignation over the US aggressions, and their violations of the basic guidelines of international law. But at present it is not so much the law at work, as the recklessness of certain military figures in the Pentagon. Now that an agreement is beginning to take shape, the Pentagon is looking for an opportunity to undermine that agreement. So it is going so far as to organize provocative airplane flights. You shot down one such plane yesterday, although you had never shot them down before when they flew over your territory. Such an action will be exploited by the aggressors for their own purposes.

For this reason we would like to offer the following friendly advice to you: show patience, restraint, and more restraint. Of course if there is an invasion, then it will be necessary to repel it with all the forces at your disposal. But do not let yourselves be provoked, since the frenzied military men in the Pentagon now, at the very moment when an elimination of the conflict is taking shape to your advantage, by including a guarantee against the invasion of Cuba, seem to want to undermine the agreement and provoke you to actions which could then be used against you. We would ask you not to let this happen. And we for our part are doing everything we can to stabilize the situation in Cuba, to protect Cuba from invasion, and to safeguard for you the possibility of the peaceful building of a socialist society.

We send our greetings to you and to all your administrative collective.

N. KHRUSHCHEV

DOCUMENT 13

Cable from USSR Ambassador to Cuba Alekseev to Soviet Ministry of Foreign Affairs, October 28, 1962[13]

In this cable to the USSR's Foreign Ministry, newly appointed Soviet ambassador to Cuba Aleksandr Alekseev reports on the perceptions of the Cuban people and leadership regarding the terms of the deal reached with Kennedy. Cuban president Dorticós informed Alekseev that the Cuban people would see the withdrawal of the missiles as a clear defeat for the Soviet Union, and that consequently, Soviet prestige would suffer. Moreover, the Cuban leadership remained skeptical about Kennedy's non-invasion pledge. Alekseev attempted to convince the Cubans that the negotiated settlement would protect the island from future U.S. aggression. The conversation between Alekseev and the Cubans reveals two very conflicting interpretations of the deal.

Upon several statements and Dorticós's reaction to N.S. Khrushchev's letter to F. Castro and to the latest message to Kennedy about the dismantling of special weaponry it became clear that confusion and bewilderment are reigning inside the Cuban leadership.

Dorticós said that, unfortunately, Cuban and Latin American peoples would perceive the decision to dismantle the special weaponry, relying only upon Kennedy's assurances, as a defeat for the Soviet government. He said that whatever assertions Kennedy made, the Cuban government could not weaken its vigilance. We understand, declared Dorticós, that this decision of the Soviet government is directed to the preserving of peace and in the end it will be advantageous for the whole socialist camp, including Cuba, but under the present conditions of great patriotic

---

13. "Cable from USSR Ambassador to Cuba Alekseev to Soviet Ministry of Foreign Affairs," October 28, 1962, History and Public Policy Program Digital Archive, Archive of Foreign Policy, Russian Federation (AVPRF), Moscow; copy obtained by NHK (Japanese Television), provided to CWIHP, and on file at National Security Archive, Washington, DC; translation by Vladimir Zaemsky, http://digitalarchive.wilsoncenter .org/document/111985.

enthusiasm of our people this report would be perceived by infinitely electrified masses as a cold shower.

He said that for the Cuban leaders the most important thing right now is to preserve the Soviet Union's prestige, which had been raised so high in Cuba. According to him, the counterrevolution will immediately seize this opportunity and direct all its work to revive distrust toward the Soviet Union. Here, said Dorticós, we must rise to the occasion in order to explain correctly to our people the meaning of the adopted decisions. He declared that under the created circumstances the Cubans were obliged to publish a statement, differing in tone from N.S. Khrushchev's letter, and there was suggested a preliminary acceptance by the Americans of the five [Cuban] conditions, including evacuation of the Guantanamo base. . . . Besides, Dorticós explained, we found ourselves in a difficult situation insofar as we had officially declared that we would not allow any UN observers on our territory. Until a certain time we will have to stick to this "maximum program" and seek ways of achieving an honorable agreement which could be reached only if we receive from the USA absolute guarantees of our security.

According to Dorticós, no Kennedy statements could be trusted inasmuch as even now the piratical flights over Cuban territory were occurring and this was done not without Kennedy's knowledge. Dorticós considers that the Americans, probably, will not stop at our consent to dismantle bases of special weapons and will demand additional concessions, in particular, the withdrawal of all the [Soviet] military units. He also showed concern about possible solution of the question of the remaining in Cuba of our military specialists and the defensive weapons at their disposal, attached for the defense of military objectives. Dorticós didn't say it openly, but permitted me to understand that the Cubans were not happy with our decision [to remove the missiles under UN inspection] undertaken without previously consulting them.

I told them that the small delay [in providing] the letter [from Khrushchev to Kennedy] was due to merely technical reasons (enciphering, transmission, translation) and made the assumption that insofar as the Cuban comrades had several times informed Moscow about the inevitability of [U.S.] intervention and bombings, probably, some quick and operational actions were needed, so there was no time for coordination. Dorticós agreed.

After my visit to Dorticós, Carlos Rafael Rodriguez came to see me (he was informed by Dorticós about the content of the letter from

N.S. Khrushchev to Fidel Castro) and presented a dismal picture of incomprehension among the Cuban people and several leaders of our decision to dismantle the special installations. He said that a lot of people think that all our specialists and their weapons would be withdrawn and they were taking it hard. According to C.R. Rodriguez, F. Castro has also reacted very painfully regarding this decision—and not the content of the decision itself because he considered it to be advantageous for mankind and the Cuban people—but the procedure of its adoption—without a previous consultation. . . . C.R. Rodriguez explained that F. Castro was defending our decision in conversations with the Cuban leaders, trying to convince them that its results would be seen later, but he had not yet found intelligible arguments for an electrified people. But the most important [thing] is that he skeptically regards Kennedy's assurances and is convinced that the Americans will go further and put forward new demands.

In my conversations with Dorticós and Rodriguez I said that, in my view, the decision on dismantling those installations did not interfere with Cuban defensive interests. It will not only save universal peace and ensure its strengthening, but this decision of the Soviet Government will eliminate the threat of invasion to Cuba and make it more difficult in the future. Regarding the issue of the incomprehension of this decision by the politically literate groups of the population, I said that this phenomenon had to be very short and the people itself would understand the wisdom of the decision and thus raise its political maturity. We are confident that Dorticós, Rodriguez, F. Castro and the majority of the [Cuban] leaders will understand correctly our decision and we will find a common language with them. Indeed, there are difficulties to explain it to the people, insofar as it has been excited beyond limits by anti-American propaganda, but we consider that there will not be serious consequences and the nearest future will prove the correctness of our decision.

DOCUMENT 14

Telegram from Soviet Deputy Foreign Minister Kuznetsov and Ambassador to the U.N. Zorin to USSR Foreign Ministry (1), October 30, 1962[14]

In this telegram to the USSR's Foreign Ministry, Soviet deputy foreign minister Vasily Kuznetsov and ambassador to the U.N. Valerian Zorin relay the substance of conversations with U.N. secretary-general U Thant. U Thant's efforts to establish an inspections regime are detailed, as are Cuban objections to such a regime. The telegram also suggests that Kennedy's non-invasion pledge will be interpreted in the narrowest sense, and that the U.S. administration will continue its attempts to undermine or overthrow Castro. The authors suggest that the remaining issues be worked out under the auspices of the U.N. Security Council and that the United Nations itself provide the framework for inspections. The document is notable for prescribing solutions that Castro would categorically reject, thereby demonstrating the gulf separating Soviet and Cuban interests.

We are communicating several thoughts on the situation that has arisen around the Cuban issue, and on our possible position and tactics in the course of future negotiations with U Thant and the Americans.

First. From talks with U Thant, conversations at the UN, and information from the American press, we have received the impression that the strategy of the USA government is at present directed towards the carrying out of our decision to dismantle military sites in Cuba, rejecting at the same time the necessity of giving clear and firm guarantees of Cuban security, restricted in this regard by the statements issued earlier by Kennedy in his messages to Comrade N.S. Khrushchev of 27 and

---

14. "Telegram from Soviet Deputy Foreign Minister Kuznetsov and Ambassador to the UN Zorin to USSR Foreign Ministry (1)," October 30, 1962, History and Public Policy Program Digital Archive, Archive of Foreign Policy, Russian Federation (AVPRF), Moscow; copy obtained by NHK (Japanese Television), provided to CWIHP, and on file at National Security Archive, Washington, DC.; translation by John Henriksen, Harvard University, http://digitalarchive.wilsoncenter.org/document/112634.

28 October, or in the last resort by the Security Council's approval of those statements. In this regard it is significant that the Americans, as is evident from available information, want the future role of the Security Council and especially of U Thant to come down basically to organizing and carrying out inspections on the dismantling of our missile installations in Cuba. As far as guarantees of Cuban security are concerned, the Americans understand that a clear and concrete resolution of the Security Council could in this respect tie their hands and keep them from proceeding with their aggressive policy toward Cuba, which it seems they do not intend to renounce. On 29 October a UPI press bulletin said that Rusk "had assured the Latin American envoys that any Soviet-American agreement would pursue the goal of the removal of missiles from Cuba, and in no way would exclude the possibility of new collective measures against Castro." In light of this, there is reason to expect that Kennedy's statement about the USA government's readiness to "give assurances that there will be no invasion of Cuba" will be interpreted by the Americans in the narrow sense, as saying that the USA and the Latin American countries will not attack Cuba with their own armed forces. At the same time they are trying to keep their hands free not only in relation to the economic blockade of Cuba and subversive operations against it, but also in their support, perhaps somewhat more disguised than earlier, for the preparation by counterrevolutionary Cuban emigres of military activities against Cuba.

Second. As far as U Thant's line is concerned, he intends, as he told us, to exchange views with Fidel Castro primarily on the issue of the verification of the dismantling of Soviet military sites, and also to ascertain that this dismantling is actually going on. On his return he intends to present a report to the Security Council precisely on these issues, after which the Council will face the practical issue of creating a monitoring apparatus. It is true that U Thant, taking into account how we put before him the issue of guarantees for Cuba, is preparing at the same time to put before Castro the issue of the so-called "UN presence" in Cuba as a guarantee of its security and a guarantee against any Cuban actions against the other Latin-American countries. In the event of the Cuban government's consenting to this sort of "UN presence" in Cuba, U Thant intends to pose the same question about a "UN presence" on the territory of the USA and certain Latin-American countries. It is however evident that the Americans will try to arrange the Security Council affair in such a way as to give priority to the issue of the mechanism for inspections on the war-site dismantling, and not to the issue of guarantees for Cuba. Moreover, U Thant's plans with regard to the guarantees for Cuba are not yet fully clear.

Third. It appears to us that in these conditions it would be expedient, in the interests of safeguarding guarantees for Cuban security, to try to bring together into one knot the main issues that must be resolved for a peaceful settlement of the Cuban crisis, most importantly the issues of control on the dismantling inspections and of guarantees for Cuba, and to reach a simultaneous settlement of these issues through the Security Council. We intend to suggest that such a resolution be given the form of a joint declaration made in the Security Council by the governments of the USSR and the USA (or by these two separately) concerning a peaceful settlement of the Cuban crisis, the Cuban government's input on this issue, and the Council's resolution approving all these declarations and entrusting the acting Secretary General of the UN, under the supervision of the Security Council, to carry out the necessary measures according to the procedures of the UN apparatus. We will propose in the framework of these declarations to stipulate, as a guarantee of Cuban security, the final end to all blockade activity against Cuba, and the duties of the USA in the capacity proposed by Comrade N.S. Khrushchev's message to Kennedy of 27 October, and taking into account Fidel Castro's statement of 28 October. If the Americans insist, we will consider the possibility of approving the explicit mention in the declaration of the Soviet government's obligation to dismantle the Soviet military sites in Cuba which the Americans call offensive, and of the Soviet government's approval of the inspection system that has been worked out. The Americans will obviously demand a declaration from the Cuban government that contains an expression of consent to the elaborated guarantees of security and of the inspection system, as well as a formulation of Cuba's non-attack obligations with regard to its neighbors, in accordance with the goals of the UN Charter. We will consult with the Cuban delegation on this issue. As far as the inspection system on the dismantling is concerned, we propose that our primary position should be to agree to the implementation of the inspections after the completion of the dismantling process. If the Americans insist on carrying out inspections during the dismantling process, it might be possible to agree to this as long as we had guarantees for a monitoring procedure that would of course keep hidden from the inspectors anything we did not want to reveal. The monitoring process should take only a short time to be carried out—only a period necessary for ascertaining that the dismantling has been completed. With regard to the composition of the inspection apparatus, there are now several variants being advanced in UN circles. According to facts released by the UN secretariat, U Thant wants to create a monitoring apparatus composed of representatives from a selection of neutral countries belonging to the UN—Sweden, Ethiopia, the United Arab Republic, Mexico, Brazil, [and] Yugoslavia, and also Switzerland. There is also an idea about delegating the monitoring process to eight neutral countries represented in the Committee on Disarmament (India, Burma, the United Arab Republic, Nigeria, Ethiopia, Mexico, Brazil, Sweden), possibly, with the goal of setting a precedent for resolving questions involving inspections on full and general disarmament. The Americans, U Thant has informed us, are putting forth a variant in which the monitoring groups consist of representatives from the USA, the USSR, and Cuba. We propose that it would be appropriate to stipulate that the monitoring groups include representatives from countries like Indonesia, Ceylon, the United Arab Republic, and Ghana. In the course of negotiations it would be possible to agree on a variant in which the groups are composed of representatives from eight neutral countries belonging to the 18th Committee on Disarmament. Furthermore a question arises about future UN measures on strengthening peace in the Caribbean region after the completion of the inspections of dismantling, and also on the inspection (by International Red Cross forces) of Soviet vessels bound for Cuba. In our opinion, it would be possible to agree to the presence in Havana (or in several Cuban commercial ports) of small groups of UN representatives (of the same composition as the groups verifying military-site dismantling) with the right to carry out selective inspections on the vessels of various countries arriving in Cuba, with the purpose of determining whether or not they are carrying so-called "offensive" sorts of armaments. [One could] make this conditional upon the requirement that the same groups of UN representatives be placed in the USA and the Latin-American countries neighboring Cuba with the right to make periodic inspections of certain regions of these countries with the purpose of determining whether preparations are being made for the invasion of Cuba, either by these countries themselves or by Cuban emigres. It would be possible to propose that this system of observation operate for the duration, for example, of one year, after which the Security Council would again examine the issue of whether a continuation of the observation is needed.

Fourth. Taking into account President Kennedy's desire, communicated through Robert Kennedy in his conversation with Comrade Dobrynin on 27 October (your #1255), we will not raise the issue of the American bases in Turkey in our negotiations with U Thant and the Americans in New York. At the same time it seems to us possible and expedient to reach an agreement with the USA that in the joint Soviet-American declaration in the Security Council, there be a record of both sides' intention to enter in the near future negotiations for normalizing relations between the NATO countries and the countries of the Warsaw Pact, as has already been outlined in the correspondence between Comrade N.S. Khrushchev and President Kennedy. In doing so it might be possible to include in such a declaration a reference both to Comrade N.S. Khrushchev's message of 28 October and Kennedy's messages of 27 and 28 October, as well as to Comrade N.S. Khrushchev's message of 27 October, in which the question about Turkey is raised.

Fifth. Until now, in our official documents and during negotiations here in New York, our weaponry now being dismantled in Cuba has been referred to as "weaponry considered offensive by the Americans." In the course of future negotiations, and especially during the preparation of the texts of the Security Council documents, we will have to oppose our own concrete formulation to the American formulation "offensive weaponry." It might be possible in our opinion to use, say, the formula "means for conveying nuclear arms at an operational distance a certain number of kilometers." All the issues laid out here will be the subject of discussions immediately after U Thant's return from Cuba, i.e., after 1 November.

DOCUMENT 15

Premier Khrushchev's Letter to Prime Minister Castro, October 30, 1962[15]

In this letter to Fidel Castro, Nikita Khrushchev attempts to smooth ruffled feathers. Particularly interesting to note is Khrushchev's

---

15. Premier Khrushchev's letter to Prime Minister Castro, October 30, 1962, reprinted from the international edition of *Granma*.

claim that he did in fact consult with Castro before reaching an agreement with Kennedy—a claim that is quite simply false. The Soviet premier also details his understanding of Castro's "Doomsday letter"; Khrushchev clearly believed that the Cuban leader "proposed that we should be the first to carry out a nuclear attack on enemy territory." Khrushchev declares that the United States "suffered a defeat" because its plans to invade Cuba were thwarted.

Esteemed Comrade Fidel Castro:

We received your letter of the 28th of October along with reports of the conversations you and President Dorticós held with our ambassador.

We comprehend your situation and take into account your difficulties during this first stage following the elimination of maximum tension that resulted from the threat of an attack by the American imperialists, one you were anticipating would come at any second.

We comprehend that certain difficulties could have come up for you as a result of the promises we made to the United States to withdraw the missile bases from Cuba in exchange for their promise to abandon their plans to invade Cuba and to prevent their allies in the Western Hemisphere from doing so, to end their so-called "quarantine"—their blockade of Cuba. This commitment led to the end of the conflict in the Caribbean, a conflict involving, as you can well understand, a confrontation between superpowers and its becoming transformed into a world war where missiles and thermonuclear weapons would have been used. According to our ambassador, some Cubans feel that the Cuban people would prefer a different kind of statement, one that didn't deal with withdrawing the missiles. It could be that these feelings exist among the people. But we, politicians and heads of state, are the leaders of the people and the people do not know everything. For that reason, we must march at the fore of the people. Thus the people will follow and respect us.

If, succumbing to popular feelings, we would have allowed ourselves to be swept along by the most aroused sectors of the populace and we would have not achieved a reasonable agreement with the US government, war would have broken out, and it would have resulted in millions of dead. The survivors would have blamed the leaders for not having taken measures to prevent this war of extermination.

Preventing war and an attack on Cuba did not just depend on the measures taken by our governments but on analysis and examination of the enemy's actions close to your territory. To put it briefly, one had to consider the situation as a whole.

Some are saying that we did not consult each other sufficiently before making the decision of which you are aware.

In reality, we consider that consultation took place, my dear Commander Fidel Castro, given that we received your wires, each one more alarming than the last, and finally your wire on October 27th where you said that you were almost certain that an attack on Cuba was imminent. According to you, it was only a matter of time: 24 or 72 hours.

When we received this very alarming wire of yours, and being aware of your courage, we believed that the warning was totally justified.

Was that not consultation with you? We interpreted that wire as a signal of maximum alarm. But had we carried out our consultations under such conditions, knowing that the warmongering and unbridled US militarists wanted to seize the occasion to attack Cuba, we would have been wasting our time and the attack would have taken place.

We believe that the presence of our strategic missiles in Cuba polarized the imperialists' attention. They were afraid that they would be used, which is why they risked wanting to eliminate them, by bombing their sites or by invading Cuba. And we have to recognize that they had the capacity to act. For that reason, I repeat, your sense of alarm was totally justified.

In your October 27th wire, you proposed that we should be the first to carry out a nuclear attack on enemy territory. Naturally, you can understand where that would have led. It wouldn't have been a simple strike but the start of a thermonuclear world war.

Dear Comrade Fidel Castro; I find your proposal to be mistaken even though I understand your reasons.

We have lived through some very serious moments; a global thermonuclear war could have broken out. Of course, the United States would have suffered enormous losses, but the Soviet Union and the entire socialist bloc would have also suffered greatly. It is difficult to say how it would have turned out for the Cuban people. First of all, Cuba would have been burned in the bonfires of war. Without a doubt the Cuban people would have fought bravely but, also without a doubt, the Cuban people would have heroically perished. We are fighting against imperialism, not to die, but to use all our potential, to lose as little as possible and to win more later on, to overcome and to see communism triumph.

The measures we have adopted have allowed us to attain the objective we established when we decided to send missiles to Cuba. We have gotten the United States to promise to not invade Cuba and to not allow its Latin American allies to do so. We have achieved all this without a nuclear war.

We believe we should take advantage of all possibilities to defend Cuba, to strengthen its Independence and sovereignty, to prevent military aggression and to avoid a thermonuclear war in this era.

And we have triumphed.

Of course, we have made concessions, we have made some compromises. We have acted under the principle of reciprocal concessions. The United States has also made concessions; it has publically promised, before the entire world, that it will not attack Cuba.

Therefore, should we compare an attack by the US and a thermonuclear war on the one hand with the compromises made on the other hand: mutual concessions, the guarantee of the inviolability of the Republic of Cuba, avoiding a world war, then I believe the conclusions are clear.

Naturally, in the defense of Cuba and other socialist countries, we cannot trust the US promise (of not invading Cuba). We have taken, and we continue taking, all necessary measures to strengthen our defenses and to accumulate the forces needed to carry out a response. At this moment, with the weapons we have given Cuba, it is capable of defending itself on its own more than ever before. Even after the dismantling of the missile bases, you possess sufficient powerful armament to drive back the enemy by land, sea and in the air close to your territory.

Furthermore, as you will remember, we stated in our message to the president of the United States on October 28th that "at the same time, we wish to assure the Cuban people that we are on their side and that we shall not abandon our responsibility to help the Cuban people". It is clear to the entire world that this is a very serious warning that we have sent to the enemy.

In meetings you stated that the US cannot be trusted. Of course you are right. Our statements on the negotiation conditions with the United States are also correct. To down a US plane over Cuban territory was a futile act, when all is said and done, because it ended without any complications. It is a lesson for the imperialists. Notwithstanding, our enemies shall interpret the events their own way. The Cuban counter-revolution will also attempt to raise its head. But we believe that you are in absolute control of the internal enemy without needing our help. The most important thing we have managed to achieve is to stop, for the time being, an attack from the external enemy.

We think that the aggressor has suffered a defeat. It was preparing an attack on Cuba but we stopped it and we have forced them to promise to the world that they shall not do it at this time. We believe this is a great victory. Of course, we also have our plans, and we shall make our decisions. This process of struggle shall go on while two socio-political systems exist on this Earth, until one of the systems, and we know it shall be our communist system, triumphs throughout the world.

Comrade Fidel Castro; we decided to send you this answer as quickly as possible. We shall make a more detailed analysis of what has occurred in a letter that we shall send you soon. In that letter we shall make a deeper analysis of the situation and give our opinion on the results of how the crisis was settled.

At this moment, negotiations for a settlement are starting and we ask you to communicate your position to us. As for us, we shall be keeping you informed on the progress of the negotiations and we shall be making all the necessary consultations.

Comrade Fidel Castro; we wish you all possible success and I am sure that you shall achieve it. There are still plots existing against you. But our intention with you is to take all the necessary steps to eliminate them and to contribute to the strengthening and development of the Cuban Revolution.

Nikita Khrushchev

DOCUMENT 16

Prime Minister Castro's Letter to Premier Khrushchev, October 31, 1962[16]

In Castro's reply to Khrushchev, he disputes the Soviet leader's claim that the Cubans were consulted about withdrawing the

---

16. Prime Minister Castro's letter to Premier Khrushchev, October 31, 1962, reprinted from international edition of *Granma*.

missiles. Castro contends that the Cuban people were ready to martyr themselves in a nuclear war with the United States; "never before," he writes, "was a people so willing to fight and die with such a universal sense of duty." It was exactly this attitude that convinced Khrushchev that the Cubans were too irrational and reckless to be entrusted with nuclear weapons.

Dear Comrade Khrushchev:

I received your letter of October 30. You understand that we indeed were consulted before you adopted the decision to withdraw the strategic missiles. You base yourself on the alarming news that you say reached you from Cuba and, finally, my cable of October 27. I don't know what news you received; I can respond for the message that I sent you the evening of October 26, which reached you the 27th.

What we did in the face of events, Comrade Khrushchev, was to prepare ourselves and get ready to fight. In Cuba there was only one kind of alarm, that of battle stations.

When in our opinion the imperialist attack became imminent I deemed it appropriate to so advise you and alert both the Soviet government and command—since there were Soviet forces committed to fight at our side to defend the Republic of Cuba from foreign aggression— about the possibility of an attack which we could not prevent but could resist.

I told you that the morale of our people was very high and that the aggression would be heroically resisted. At the end of the message I reiterated to you that we awaited the events calmly.

Danger couldn't impress us, for danger has been hanging over our country for a long time now and in a certain way we have grown used to it.

The Soviet troops which have been at our side know how admirable the stand of our people was throughout this crisis and the profound brotherhood that was created among the troops from both peoples during the decisive hours. Countless eyes of Cuban and Soviet men who were willing to die with supreme dignity shed tears upon learning about the surprising, sudden and practically unconditional decision to withdraw the weapons.

Perhaps you don't know the degree to which the Cuban people were ready to do its duty toward the nation and humanity.

I realized when I wrote them that the words contained in my letter could be misinterpreted by you and that was what happened, perhaps because you didn't read them carefully, perhaps because of the translation, perhaps because I meant to say so much in too few lines. However, I didn't hesitate to do it. Do you believe, Comrade Khrushchev, that we were selfishly thinking of ourselves, of our generous people willing to sacrifice themselves, and not at all in an unconscious manner but fully assured of the risk they ran?

No, Comrade Khrushchev. Few times in history, and it could even be said that never before, because no people had ever faced such a tremendous danger, was a people so willing to fight and die with such a universal sense of duty.

We knew, and do not presume that we ignored it, that we would have been annihilated, as you insinuate in your letter, in the event of nuclear war. However, that didn't prompt us to ask you to withdraw the missiles, that didn't prompt us to ask you to yield. Do you believe that we wanted that war? But how could we prevent it if the invasion finally took place? The fact is that this event was possible, that imperialism was obstructing every solution and that its demands were, from our point of view, impossible for the USSR and Cuba to accept.

And if war had broken out, what could we do with the insane people who unleashed the war? You yourself have said that under current conditions such a war would inevitably have escalated quickly into a nuclear war.

I understand that once aggression is unleashed, one shouldn't concede to the aggressor the privilege of deciding, moreover, when to use nuclear weapons. The destructive power of this weaponry is so great and the speed of its delivery so great that the aggressor would have a considerable initial advantage.

And I did not suggest to you, Comrade Khrushchev, that the USSR should be the aggressor, because that would be more than incorrect, it would be immoral and contemptible on my part. But from the instant the imperialists attack Cuba and while there are Soviet armed forces stationed in Cuba to help in our defense in case of an attack from abroad, the imperialists would by this act become aggressors against Cuba and against the USSR, and we would respond with a strike that would annihilate them.

Everyone has his own opinions and I maintain mine about the dangerousness of the aggressive circles in the Pentagon and their preference for a preventive strike. I did not suggest, Comrade Khrushchev, that in the midst of this crisis the Soviet Union should attack, which is what your letter seems to say; rather, that following an imperialist attack, the USSR should act without vacillation and should never make the mistake of allowing circumstances to develop in which the enemy makes the first nuclear strike against the USSR. And in this sense, Comrade Khrushchev, I maintain my point of view, because I understand it to be a true and just evaluation of a specific situation. You may be able to convince me that I am wrong, but you can't tell me that I am wrong without convincing me.

I know that this is a delicate issue that can only be broached in circumstances such as these and in a very personal message.

You may wonder what right I have to broach this topic. I do so without worrying about how thorny it is, following the dictates of my conscience as a revolutionary duty and inspired by the most unselfish sentiments of admiration and affection for the USSR, for what she represents for the future of humanity and by the concern that she should never again be the victim of the perfidy and betrayal of aggressors, as she was in 1941, and which cost so many lives and so much destruction. Moreover, I spoke not as the troublemaker but as a combatant from the most endangered trenches.

I do not see how you can state that we were consulted in the decision you took.

I would like nothing more than to be proved wrong at this moment. I only wish that you were right.

There are not just a few Cubans, as has been reported to you, but in fact many Cubans who are experiencing at this moment unspeakable bitterness and sadness.

The imperialists are talking once again of invading our country, which is proof of how ephemeral and untrustworthy their promises are. Our people, however, maintain their indestructible will to resist the aggressors and perhaps more than ever need to trust in themselves and in that will to struggle.

We will struggle against adverse circumstances, we will overcome the current difficulties and we will come out ahead, and nothing can destroy the ties of friendship and the eternal gratitude we feel toward the USSR.

Fraternally,
Fidel Castro

DOCUMENT 17

Meeting of the Secretary of the Communist Party of Cuba with Mikoyan in the Presidential Palace, November 4, 1962[17]

During this meeting between Cuban leaders and Anastas Mikoyan, who was sent to Havana to smooth things over with Castro, a number of important issues are discussed, including the significance of the Cuban Revolution to the socialist bloc, the principles of Marxism-Leninism, and military interventionism in Latin America. Mikoyan explains that the purpose of the missiles was not to improve the strategic situation of the USSR, but to contain U.S. aggression by providing a deterrent, and empha-sizes that all measures taken by the Soviets were for the purpose of protecting Cuba. The conversation is noteworthy because it reveals the differences in opinion between the Soviets and the Cubans, and lays out the official Soviet party line regarding the outcome of the missile crisis.

Preamble by Mikoyan:

He says he has come to Cuba to discuss their differences with the Cuban Companeros [comrades] and not to [discuss] what has been stated by the imperialists. They trust us as much as they trust themselves. He is willing to discuss for as long as it takes to solve the differences. The interests of the Soviet Union are common to ours in the defense of the principles of Marxism-Leninism and in all the other interests.

FIDEL: Summarizes our differences in terms of the procedures used to deal with this crisis.

DORTICOS: Asks whether Mikoyan considers that they have obtained the guarantees that president Kennedy offered.

---

17. "Meeting of the Secretary of the Communist Party of Cuba with Mikoyan in the Presidential Palace," November 4, 1962, History and Public Policy Program Digital Archive, Institute of History, Cuba, obtained and provided by Philip Brenner (American University). Translation from Spanish by Carlos Osorio (National Security Archive), http://digitalarchive.wilsoncenter.org/document/110879.

CARLOS: Asks whether the victory mentioned by the Soviets has been attained.

MIKOYAN: Says he will respond to the questions, and asks to be excused for he will speak for a long time. He says he will start with the doubts expressed by Fidel in order to explain them.

He thinks that the main problem consists in explaining why they have sent troops and strategic weapons. If this is not understood, it is very difficult to understand the whole situation. He did not think we had doubts about this. He said that "the fate of the Cuban revolution is a permanent preoccupation of ours, especially since its socialist character was declared. When the imperialists were defeated in Girón [Bay of Pigs], we congratulated ourselves, but we also worried. The Yankees did a stupid thing but we knew they would continue harassing because Cuba is an example that they could not tolerate. Our assessment was that they had two parallel plans; the first one consisted of the economic strangulation of Cuba in order to bring down the regime without a military intervention. The second one consisted of an intervention organized by Latin American governments and their support, as an alternative to the other plan.

We consider the victory of the Cuban revolution as an enormous contribution to Marxism-Leninism. Its defeat would be an irreparable damage to Marxism and to other revolutionary movements in other countries. Such a defeat would mean the preponderance of imperialism over socialism in the world. Such a defeat would mean a terrible blow against the world revolution. It would break the correlation of forces. It is our duty to do everything possible to defend Cuba.

Our comrades told us that the economic situation in Cuba had worsened due to the Yankees' pressure and the enormous military expenses. This worried us for it coincided with the plans of the Yankees. We had a discussion about the economic decline and we have helped without you requesting it. You are very modest in your requests and we try to help you. We decided to give you weapons for free and donated equipment for 100,000 men. In addition, in our commercial negotiations, we have looked at all the possibilities and we have tried to provide everything you needed without payments in kind. We have given you 180 million rubles in order to help you. This is a second phase of help because before that there were commercial and credit agreements but these last deliveries have been in aid.

When Khrushchev visited Bulgaria [May 14–May 20, 1962] he expressed many things to us, he said, "although I was in Bulgaria, I was always thinking of Cuba. I fear the Yankees will attack Cuba, directly or indirectly, and imagine of the effect on us of the defeat of the Cuban revolution. We cannot allow this to happen. Although the plan is very risky for us, it is a big responsibility for it exposes us to a war. Cuba must be saved." They thought it over for three days and later all the members of the Central Committee expressed their opinions. We have to think a lot about this action in order to save Cuba and not to provoke a nuclear war. He ordered the military to develop the Plan and to consult with the Cubans. He told us that the main condition was to carry out the Plan secretly. Our military told us that four months were needed for the preparations. We thought the enemy would learn about it right in the middle of the plan and we anticipated what to do. We thought the plan would not be carried out to the end, but this was an advantage, for the troops would already be on the Island. We foresaw that, in order not to provoke a war, we could use the UNO [United Nations Organization] and the public opinion. We thought the Plan would not provoke a war but a blockade against weapons and fuel instead. How to solve this—your lack of fuel? Considering the geographic situation of the Island, it has been very difficult to avoid the blockade. If you were closer we could have used our Air Force and our Fleet, but we could not. The Yankees do have bases surrounding us in Turkey and blocking the Black Sea. Given the situation, we cannot strike back. Okinawa is too far away too. The only possibility was to cut the communications with West Berlin. In Berlin this is possible.

We have not thought of building a Soviet Base on the Island to operate against the North Americans. In general, we consider that the policy of bases is not a correct one. We only have bases in [East] Germany, first because of the right we have as an invading country, and after that due to the Warsaw Treaty. . . . In the past, we have had them in Finland and in China too (Port Arthur)—those bases we have abandoned. We only have troops in Hungary and Poland, to protect the troops in Germany and the communications with Austria.

We do not need bases to destroy the United States because we can attack with the missiles deployed in our territory. We do not have a plan to conquer North America. The only thing we need to do is to launch a counter strike, but that will serve to destroy them without having to send in our troops.

We have sent the troops and strategic missiles only to protect the Island's defense. It was a plan of containment so that the Yankees could not provoke an explosion in Cuba. If the missiles are well camouflaged and the Yankees do not know where they are deployed, then they can help to contain them. The military told us that they could be well hidden in the palm forests of Cuba. The Yankees were not going to locate them. They could not destroy them. During July and August, they did not find anything, it was not until October that they have been found. We were surprised that Kennedy only made reference to technicians and not to our troops. At first, it seems that that is what he thought. Later we learned that he knew more than he was saying, but he was not revealing it [so as] not to hinder the electoral campaign. We let the Yankees know that we were going to solve the Berlin problem, in order to distract their attention from the other problem. We did not intend to act on Berlin. I can explain this later.

It was known through diplomatic channels that Kennedy did not want to make matters more serious and asked us not to move on the issue of Berlin before the elections. We told him that we agreed to this. We would please him and we would solve it later. We thought it was convenient to please him. In addition, we had not thought of bringing up this problem. When the North Americans learned about the transports to Cuba, they also concentrated their campaign on Berlin. Both sides had their principal interest in Cuba, but appeared as if concentrated on Berlin. In the middle of October, they [the North Americans] learned about it through Cuba, via the West Germany information service who passed it to the CIA, they first learned about the missiles. They took aerial pictures and located them. Khrushchev ordered that the missiles be laid down during the day and that they be raised only during the night. Evidently, this order was never carried out. Kennedy did not want to talk about the missiles until the end of the elections. But two Republican Senators learned the news and they had no alternative but to act. We did not know what Kennedy would do and we worried about the preparations or maneuvers of . . . an operation named after Castro but backwards. When Kennedy talked about the blockade, we did not have data showing whether it was a maneuver or a preparation for aggression. On the morning of the 28th we received the news confirming that it was an aggression. Although it was announced that the maneuvers were suspended due to a storm, the storm was over and the maneuvers were not carried out. In the meantime, the concentration continued. Khrushchev has strongly criticized Kennedy's words about the blockade. They did not approve of the kind of weapons that Cuba should own and thus they organized a direct aggression. Their plan consisted of two parts: using missiles with conventional loads to destroy the nuclear missiles and then landing and destroying the resistance.

In case of the latter, we would be forced to respond because it is an attack against Cuba and against us too—because our troops were here and this was the unleashing of the World War. We would destroy North America. They would inflict huge losses on us; but they would make every effort to destroy Cuba completely. All the measures we took were taken to protect Cuba. What would have been the result if the plan of the Yankees was carried out? Lose Cuba, inflict enormous damages upon the Socialist countries with a nuclear war? While we were in the midst of our discussions, we received a cable from Fidel that coincided with other information in the same vein. After that, ten to twelve hours were left. Given that such a short time was left, we used diplomatic channels. Because when policy-makers want to avoid a war, they have to use diplomatic means. It's important to underscore that Kennedy says now that he was not against the presence of troops here and that he accepts ground-to-air missiles. But once known, the strategic weapons, were not useful anymore....

The withdrawal of the missiles, was a concession on our part. But Kennedy also makes a concession by permitting the Soviet weapons [to remain in Cuba], in addition, declaring that they will not attack Cuba nor permit that it be attacked. In assessing the outcome, we have gained, because they will not attack Cuba and there will be no war.

In normal conditions, it would be natural that we send you a draft for you to study and you could then publish it. But that can be done only in normal conditions. An invasion was expected within the next 24 hours. When Fidel sent his cable, there were only ten to twelve hours left. If a cable was sent it had to have been encrypted, that would take more than 10 to 12 hours. Consultations would have been appropriate, but Cuba would not exist and the world would be enveloped in a war. After the attack, they would have never accepted a truce, due to the warmongers of the Pentagon. Our attitude has produced difficulties, but in making an overall evaluation, in spite of the psychological defects, we can see that the advantages are undeniable.

Dorticos asks: What guarantees offered by Kennedy have really been obtained? We consider that all agreements cannot be rejected in a nihilistic fashion. Although agreements can be breached, they are important for they are useful for a certain period of time.

In addition, a problem arose with the Turkey issue. [Mikoyan said:] Why did we include the problem of Turkey and the bases? We did not have in our plans to discuss Turkey; but while we were discussing that issue, we received an article from [U.S. journalist Walter] Lip[p]man[n] saying that the Russians will discuss that, [and] that is why we included it. The bases in Turkey are of no importance because in case of war they would be destroyed. There are also bases in England that could damage all the bases anywhere in the world.

Fidel asks whether there were in fact two letters [from Khrushchev to Kennedy], one that mentioned the issue of Turkey, which was broadcast on Radio Moscow, and another in which the issue was not mentioned. [Mikoyan replied:] We sent two letters, one on the 26th that was not published, and another one on the 27th. The issue of Turkey was not included at the beginning, we included it later. But we can describe all that in more detail through a reviewing of the documents. We have had discussions about your question whether the dismantling of the base at Guantanamo is better. That would be better for Cuba, but from a military point of view of the interest of Cuba, it is not possible. If we decided to withdraw all the weapons from Cuba, then we could demand the withdrawal from Guantanamo, Guantanamo has no importance in military terms. That would be more dangerous, and that is important from a political perspective. Concerning the inspection: if we said we reject any inspection, the enemy could interpret that as an attempt to trick them. All it is about is seeing the sites, where the weapons were and their shipping for a few days. Cuba is in the hands of the Cubans. But because we were the owners of those weapons . . . [paragraph missing]. We thought that you, after the consultations, you would accept the inspection. But we never thought of deciding anything for you. Why did we think that we could accept a verification of the dismantling by neutrals, without infringement of the Cuban sovereignty? It was understood that no State would accept an infringement of your sovereignty. . . .

We spoke about the problem of dismantling with [U.S. negotiator John J.] McCloy in New York. . . . I talked to them about the aerial photographic inspection, but I responded that Cuba has the right to its air space. I told them that their planes have flown over Cuba and they were convinced that the dismantling is being carried out. They admitted that, but pointed out that not everything is finished. We told them that this is nearly completed and he did not talk further about it. [McCloy said:] We have to be sure that they are not going to hide them in the forest. We do not want data pertaining to your military secrets; but we need assurances that the missiles will go.

We can provide the pictures of the dismantled weapons and how they are loaded. Nor will we oppose that you observe the ships on the high seas, at a particular distance. They (or you) will see something on the decks. I did not tell them that, but that is our opinion and we will provide them with the materials to convince them that we have withdrawn the missiles. So we will not contradict your [Cuban] declaration, against the inspection or the aerial verification. They feared that the Cubans would not allow us to withdraw the missiles, given that they have 140,000 and you only have 10,000 men. I did not talk about these numbers. He said that the U-2 that was shot down here, was shot at with Russian missiles and probably operated by Russians. Although they think there may be Cubans who are able to operate those weapons. We kept on insisting that they lift the quarantine immediately. I told them that if they wanted the missiles withdrawn faster, they should lift the blockade. Because the ships that are now in Cuba are not able to take those missiles out. I told them they should issue instructions so that the inspection of the ships be carried out without anybody boarding the ships. It would rather be carried out in a symbolic manner, asking by radio, as it was done with the tanker Bucharest.

Stevenson said they will accept the proposals of U Thant. We reproached him that he proposed not to bring weapons to Cuba and to lift the blockade. We have complied with this and they continue.

We have losses because the ships wait on the high seas. The losses are considerable, that is why we have allowed the control of the Red Cross. The Red Cross is better because it is not a political institution, nor a governmental institution. U Thant proposed two inspections, one at the shipping harbors and another on the high seas. Not wanting to hurt his feelings, we responded that we accept the inspection on the high seas and not at the shipping harbors.

U Thant, when returning from Cuba, told me that you did not agree, although this verification is easier at the harbors. U Thant is ready, he is choosing the personnel and has already two ships. I do not know more about it, for it is [Soviet deputy foreign minister V. V.] Kuznetsov who deals with this issue.

In this situation, Thant has played a good role. You cannot ask more, given his situation, he even seems to have a little sympathy for our position. While in Moscow, we received a plan of guarantees. We thought this plan seemed interesting and useful for Cuba. Why: If the inspection of Cuba, the southern coast of the U.S. and other countries in the Caribbean will be approved because this way you deprive the aggressor of the possibility to carry out its goals. Of course, this can be circumvented, however. I have been interested in this variant from another point of view. There is an OAS [Organization of American States], and it is the U.S. who profits from it instead of using the UN. But if this plan is approved, it is the UNO that will deal with this part of the American Continent, this constitutes a blow to the Monroe Doctrine. U Thant said that the representatives from Latin American countries agree with this plan, the North Americans avoid responding to it. I asked McCloy and he said at the beginning (as did Stevenson) that the U Thant Plan does not exist. But afterward they discarded the U.S. inspection and they said they can give their word that in Latin America all the camps [of anti-Castro Cuban exiles] are liquidated. I asked him if all were, and he avoided the question. They said that Cuba was a revolutionary infection, he said that the Latin American countries fear Cuba. A formula can be searched in which Cuba will abandon the clandestine work in exchange for their not attacking.

Fidel was right when he said that it's easier for the USSR to maneuver and maintain a flexible policy than it is for Cuba, all the more as the Yankee radio reaches Cuba easily. It is not just to say that we are more liberal. The Cuban revolution cannot be lost. You have to maneuver to save the Revolution by being flexible.

In retrospect the question that arises is whether it was a mistake to send the missiles and then withdraw them from the Island. Our Central Committee says that this is not a mistake. We consider that the missiles did their job by making Cuba the focus of the world diplomacy. After they were captured in photos, they cannot accomplish their role of containment.

In Latin America no country has the power that Cuba has. No Latin American bloc can defeat Cuba.

In order to understand on what victory rests, you may compare the situation of Cuba now and four months ago. The first advantage is that the North Americans stopped talking about the Monroe Doctrine and before, the whole basis for their policy toward Latin America was that doctrine.

Before, they declared they would not tolerate the existence of a Marxist-Leninist regime in Latin America, now they declare that they will not attack Cuba. Before they did not tolerate a country from abroad in the Caribbean and now they know of the existence of Soviet specialists and do not say a thing.

Before, you could not have any action of the UN in favor of Cuba and now it is working in that sense, all the peoples are mobilized.

The prestige of the Socialist Camp has grown because it defended peace. Although the United States brought the world to the brink of a war, the USSR, by pacific means, was able to save Cuba and the peace.

Peace has been secured for several years and Cuba must be consolidated for it to continue building socialism and continue being the Lighthouse for Latin America.

The prestige of Cuba has grown as a consequence of these events.

DOCUMENT 18

Brazilian Foreign Ministry Memorandum, "Question of Cuba," November 20, 1962[18]

This memorandum from the Brazilian foreign minister, Jorge Alberto Seixas Corrêa, provides a Latin American perspective on the crisis. It should be noted that the president of Brazil at this time was a progressive reformer, João Goulart, who responded to the crisis by spearheading efforts to declare Latin America a nuclear-free zone. According to the Brazilians, the United States had achieved most of its goals, while the Soviet Union was facing difficulties with its Cuban ally. The Brazilians put forward a modest plan for attaining lasting peace in the region.

Question of Cuba

Permit me Your Excellency to recapitulate, in a manner more succinct and focused, only, on aspects of the question that interest the aims of the

18. "Brazilian Foreign Ministry Memorandum, 'Question of Cuba,'" November 20, 1962, History and Public Policy Program Digital Archive, Ministry of External Relations Archives, Brasilia, Brazil, copy courtesy of Roberto Baptista Junior (History Department, University of Brasilia). Translation from Portuguese by James G. Hershberg, http://digitalarchive.wilsoncenter.org/document/115317.

present Memorandum, the current development of the Cuban crisis, in that it refers particularly to the three parties directly involved—United States of America, USSR and Cuba.

I—UNITED STATES OF AMERICA

2. In that which concerns the United States of America, it appears to have fully attained the objective of its naval and aerial blockade, which was to impede the entry, to Cuba, of warlike material of an offensive nature. Moreover, even, the Soviet Union agreed to withdraw, or dismantle, sur place, the armaments which had been installed on Cuban territory, under its control. On the other hand, in the bilateral negotiations that have been between the United States of America and the USSR, the Washington government gave guarantees of non-invasion of Cuba.

3. To reach a final solution to the Cuban question, the American Government, still, demands: a) the withdrawal by the Soviets, of additional armaments—long-range bombers—b) the inspection, by an international group, on Cuban territory, of the works of dismantling and withdrawal of the offensive and nuclear war material. As for the first demand, Moscow alleged that it is not a fitting initiative in the matter, since the planes at issue have already been incorporated into the Cuban air force. In this case, the Government of Cuba has to agree to return to the Soviet Union the machines at issue.

II—U.S.S.R.

4. Beyond the direct action of the USSR in the question, already mentioned in previous paragraphs, there is to consider the current position of the government of Premier Khrushchev, in view of the information received by the Embassy in Moscow.

5. Ambassador Leitão da Cunha commented on the immediate effects that the events in the Caribbean have had regarding the line of foreign policy of Moscow. It appears to have fixed on a new idea of "compromise," in solution of international disputes in which the Soviet Union is a direct party. Still according to Ambassador Leitão da Cunha, the line followed by Khrushchev of "peaceful coexistence" has undergone a change of direction, which approximates the Brazilian idea of "competitive coexistence."

6. This new philosophy was not adopted without the Soviet Premier having to overcome obstacles, in front of difficulties and criticisms, above all on the part of its more radical allies. The current intransigence of Fidel

Castro to gestures of Mikoyan, causes discomfort in the Soviet environment. On the other hand, it has inspired that he will be—certainly he is—in egotistical motives and of the momentary strategy, the current attitude of Khrushchev has been conciliatory, pacific, and, evidently, all solutions should be searched that would not put them to lose ground already conquered or compromise future negotiations.

III—CUBA

7. Pressured by the Soviets, Fidel Castro has ready now conformed in abdicating certain demands that he initially made—withdrawal of the Americans of the naval base of Guantanamo—as conditions for agreeing with an international inspection on his territory. The most recent communications received from our Embassy in Havana permit one to deduce, that the government of Fidel Castro is disposed to accept an international solution for the question, within which would be, in part, protecting his prestige next to the Cuban people. It may not be, therefore, that he would be lead to assume a position of intransigence, compromising irremediably the conciliatory solution that he searches to reach.

8. In these conditions, and on a merely speculative basis—a time that, as is natural in case, there is not the DAS, up to date with the intentions of the Government, in that it respects its direct and future participation in the unrolling of the events in the Caribbean—permit me to recall to Your Excellency the possibility of Brazil suggesting the path of a conciliatory solution for the question of Cuba, in which would participate the Governments of the United States of America, the Soviet Union and of Havana.

9. The idea would be to launch in an informal manner, for example, in an interview granted by the Mr. Minister of State with a highly-regarded foreign correspondent. It would not assume the form of an offer of good offices or of mediation on the part of Brazil, but an indication of a formula that all would be able to accept. Another form of action in this sense would be of a gesture together or isolated on the part of Latin American Governments that maintain diplomatic relations with Fidel Castro.

10. Such a solution would consist in the mentioned Governments assuming a commitment of "negative obligations."

11. Already on the occasion of examining the matters that would be tackled by President João Goulart and Kennedy, was thought of a high

hierarchy in this Case that the attitude in front of the Cuban Government that would bear better fruits for the community of the Hemisphere would be for them to realize gestures together to Fidel Castro in the sense of assuming negative obligations, instead of following the path of isolation of Cuba, and of reprisals.

12. In synthesis, this compromise, that would be the object of a formal declaration, together or isolated, of the three interested Governments, would extend to the following negative obligations:

on the part of the United States of America:

—not to intervene, directly or indirectly, in Cuba.

on the part of the Soviet Union:

I—not to supply offensive armament to Cuba.

II—not to intervene, directly or indirectly, in Cuba.

on the part of Cuba:

I—not to install offensive armament.

II—not to intervene, directly or indirectly, in the politics, of other countries of the continent.

13. The suspension of the naval and aerial blockade of Cuba, on the part of the United States, as well as agreement of the Havana Government to withdraw the bomber aircraft and in relation to inspection by an international commission, is obvious, precedes the formalization of such a compromise or there will be a concomitant process.

14. The initiative of the Brazilian Government on the above lines indicate that it would be perfectly coherent with its position toward the events in the Caribbean, and, more still, would present an opportunity for us to reaffirm certain principles that guide our foreign policy in the hemisphere; the self-determination of peoples; the opposition to armed methods; and the rejection of infiltration and imposition of political ideology to our democratic system.

Respectfully,
Jorge Alberto Seixas Corrêa

DOCUMENT 19

Letter from Khrushchev to Fidel Castro, January 31, 1963[19]

In this letter to Castro, Khrushchev attempts to patch up relations between the Soviet Union and Cuba. He attempts to convince Castro that the Kennedy administration's non-invasion pledge represented a major victory for the socialist bloc, and that the Cuban Revolution would be protected from future U.S. aggression. He also invites Castro for an extended visit to Moscow. Castro accepted the offer, and the visit was used not just to repair the Soviet-Cuban alliance, but also to demonstrate to the rest of the world that the missile crisis had not destroyed the friendship between the two countries.

Dear Comrade Fidel Castro,

I have been thinking of writing this letter to you for a long time now. And now that I am on my way back to Moscow from Berlin, where I was attending the congress of the Socialist Party of Germany, I am writing this letter to you. Our train is passing through the fields and forests of Soviet Belorussia, and it occurred to me suddenly that it would be very nice if you yourself could take a look, now in this sunny weather, at the earth covered with snow, at the forests covered with frost. You are a man from the South, you must have seen this only in pictures. It is probably difficult for you to imagine what the ground looks like when it is covered with white trees and the forests when they are covered with white frost. And it would be nice if you could see our country during all the seasons of the year. In our country every season—spring, summer, autumn, and winter—has its own delights! . . . But all these ramblings about nature should not distract me from the main subject of this letter. The main point here is the deep wish felt by me and my friends to meet with you, to talk a little, to have a heart-to-heart chat. We have things to talk about.

---

19. "Letter from Khrushchev to Fidel Castro," January 31, 1963, History and Public Policy Program Digital Archive, Archive of Foreign Policy, Russian Federation (AVPRF), http://digitalarchive.wilsoncenter.org/document/114507.

I would like this meeting and this conversation not to be postponed for long. I would like our meeting to take place soon.

Why so soon? Well, because you and we have survived a very important period, a period that will be considered a milestone in the development of Cuba, of the Soviet Union, and of all socialist countries. After all, we are the first countries after the Second World War to come so close to war. And at the center of this dangerous crisis in the Caribbean Sea was Cuba. We understand that most of the urgency of the crisis has been eliminated by now, but even so the danger of the encounter has not completely disappeared. You understand this very well, and we fully share your concern, and are evaluating the situation with it in mind.

But what is most important now is the question: Why should we need to meet with you and talk openly? The urgency of the crisis that was created by American imperialism in the Caribbean Sea area has been eliminated. But it seems to me that that crisis has left behind some trace, albeit hardly perceptible, in the relations between our states—Cuba and the Soviet Union—and in our personal relations. Now, to speak quite honestly, they are not what they used to be before the crisis. I will hide that fact that this saddens and worries us. And it seems to me that in many ways the future growth of our relations depends on a meeting between us. At the present time, a means of contact such as written correspondence simply is not sufficient. Nothing can replace a personal conversation. After all, in conversation any misunderstanding of each other's positions can be easily and quickly corrected, and a common language can be found. Thus people who use technical means for getting together and exchanging opinions try to have personal meetings, personal contacts, and personal conversations. As you know, our enemies meet quite frequently, perhaps even more frequently than we do. And you and we should meet with each other.

During the crisis in the Caribbean Sea, our views did not always coincide, we gave different evaluations to the various stages of that crisis, and we had somewhat different approaches to finding ways to eliminate it. After our well-known statement, you even said publicly that during the unfolding of the crisis a certain discord had arisen between the Soviet government and the government of Cuba. As you yourself understand, this did not make us happy. And now that the tension has eased and we have entered a different phase of relations between Cuba and the

Soviet Union—on the one hand we have a different relationship with the United States of America, and on the other band, there also remain some fissures (how deep they are is difficult to determine) in the relations between us and Cuba.

Thus we want a meeting, at which time we would be able to bridge up and eliminate those fissures between us, however deep they may be; they may even simply be light marks which could be easily erased. There should be no rough patches in the relations between our two socialist countries. Our relations should be truly brotherly.

DOCUMENT 20

"I Know Something About the Caribbean Crisis," Notes from a Conversation with Fidel Castro, November 5, 1987[20]

In this memorandum of conversation between Fidel Castro and Georgy Shakhnazarov, the deputy chairman of the Central Committee department responsible for relations with Cuba, Castro reveals his thoughts and memories of the missile crisis. Particularly interesting is his recollection that he wanted the arms deal with the Soviets to be public, and that he was unable to get a clear answer about the purpose of the secret deal. Castro believes that regardless of Khrushchev's assurances about the primary purpose of the missiles being to defend the Cuban Revolution, the strategic implications of the weapons were at the forefront of the Soviet premier's considerations. Castro also claims that he was hesitant at first to accept the deal, as he did not want to be seen as establishing a Soviet military base in Cuba, and that at the time he agreed to receive the weapons, he was unaware of

---

20. "I Know Something About the Caribbean Crisis," notes from a conversation with Fidel Castro, November 5, 1987, Cold War International History Project Bulletin, Issue 5, Spring 1995, pp. 87–89, available at http://www.latinamericanstudies.org/cold-war /castro-speech-1968.pdf.

the actual balance of military power and did not know how many missiles the Soviet Union had.

In October [1962] the American planes began low flights above the Soviet launching sites for the nuclear intermediate range missiles and the anti-aircraft launchers. At that time the antiaircraft missiles had the range of more than 1,000 meters. Paired ground-to-air launchers were used for protection of those anti-aircraft launchers, but they could not provide effective protection. We gave an order to add hundreds of additional anti-aircraft launchers to protect those launchers. Additional launchers were in the Cuban hands. That way we wanted to protect the Soviet nuclear and anti-aircraft missiles that were deployed in Cuba. Low overflights by the American planes represented a real threat of an unexpected attack on those objects. At my meeting with the Commander-in-chief of the Soviet forces in Cuba [Gen. I. A. Pliyev] I raised the question of the serious danger that the American overflights represented. That meeting occurred on the 25th or the 26th. I told him that the Cuban side could not allow the American planes to fly at such low altitudes over the Cuban territory any more. I even sent a letter [dated October 26] to Khrushchev about that. In that letter I told the Soviet leader about my concern with the situation that had developed. I said that we should not allow the Americans to deliver a first strike at the Soviet objects in the Cuban territory, we should not allow the repetition of the events that led to the World War II. At that time the crisis situation already existed.

On the day when the American planes appeared again, we gave orders to all Cuban antiaircraft batteries to fire. The planes were driven off by the defensive fire. However, not a single plane had been shot down. Later on the same day [October 27] a spying plane, U-2, appeared in the air above the island. We don't know any details, but it happened so that the plane was shot down by a Soviet anti-aircraft missile over the eastern part of the country.

I don't know in what manner they reported that to Khrushchev and to the General Staff of the Soviet armed forces, however, I doubt that the order to shoot down the plane was given by the Commander-in-Chief of the Soviet troops in Cuba [Pliyev]; that decision was most probably made by the commander of the anti-aircraft missiles, or even by a commander of one of the batteries. Khrushchev, however, accused us of shooting down that plane in his letter.

To be sincere, it was possible that we were to blame since we opened fire at the American planes first, because we were so decisively against the American overflights. But the biggest mistake probably was that you, having installed those missiles, still allowed the Americans to fly over the launching sites. Those overflights were nothing else but preparation for a sudden American invasion of Cuba. I cannot blame the Soviet comrade who shot the U-2 for what he did because I understand his psychological condition very well. He saw that the Cubans opened fire at the American planes, and he decided to fire a missile at the U-2. I heard that many years later he was decorated for that act.

It is interesting that the former Soviet Ambassador in Cuba, [Aleksandr] Alekseev, wrote in his memoirs that I was trying to avoid the collision. For the sake of historical objectivity I must say that that was not so. In my letter to Khrushchev after we had deployed the anti-aircraft batteries and mobilized our people to repel the aggression I expressed my hope that we would be able to preserve peace. I wanted to show Khrushchev that I was not in an aggressive mood. At the same time I wanted to inform him about my concern with the possibility of an American first strike, not even excluding a possibility of a nuclear strike against Cuba.

At the same time I suggested to the Soviet Commander-in-Chief in Cuba [Pliyev] to disperse the nuclear warheads, so that they would not have been completely destroyed in case of an American attack. And he agreed with me.

One more question concerned the public statements made by the Soviet leadership and the coverage of the events in the organs of mass media. I sent two emissaries to Moscow [on August 27–September 2, 1962]—I think they were Che Guevara and [Emilio] Aragones—who had to propose that Khrushchev make public the military agreement between the USSR and Cuba. Publicly the Soviet leaders claimed that there were no offensive weapons in Cuba. I insisted that we should not allow the Americans to speculate with the public opinion, that we should make the agreement public. However, Khrushchev declined.

The American leaders, Kennedy in particular, reacted to the Soviet statements very negatively. They thought they were deceived.

We, however, never denied the presence of the Soviet missiles in Cuba. In all their public statements Cuban representatives stated that the question of presence of weapons in Cuba was a sovereign business of the Cuban people, that we had the right to use any kind of weapons for the defense of the revolution. We believed that those statements of the Soviet leaders did harm to the prestige of the Soviet Union in the eyes of the general public, since at the same time you allowed U-2 flights over the Cuban territory that took pictures of the missiles stationed there.

At that time the question of the withdrawal of the Soviet missiles had not been raised yet. However, the aggravation of the situation forced Khrushchev to make that decision. We, on our part, thought that Khrushchev had rushed, having made that decision without any consultation with us. We believe that the inclusion of the Cuban side in the negotiations would have made it possible to get bigger concessions from the Americans, possibly including the issue of the American base in Guantanamo. Such rush resulted in the fact that we found out about the Soviet-American agreement from the radio. Moreover, the first statement said that American missiles would be withdrawn only from Turkey; in the second the mentioning of Turkey was dropped.

When I visited the Soviet Union in 1963, Khrushchev read several letters to me. The American letters were signed by Thompson, but the real author was Robert Kennedy. In Khrushchev's response he spoke about the missiles in Turkey and Italy. There were certain threats in Kennedy's letter. In particular, he wrote that if the Russians did not accept their proposals, something would have happened. In response to that Khrushchev stated that something would have happened indeed if the Americans undertook any actions against Cuba in disregard of the agreement, and that that something would have been incredible in its scale. That meant that if the Americans had dared to violate the agreement, a war would have begun.

Probably Khrushchev did not anticipate that the interpreter who read the originals would have mentioned Italy, but the original letter mentioned the withdrawal of missiles from Turkey and Italy. Later I asked the Soviet side to give explanations of that issue, but they told me that the agreement mentioned only Turkey.

We couldn't help being disappointed by the fact that even though the Soviet part of the agreement talked only about the missiles in Cuba and did not mention other types of weapons, particularly IL-28 planes, subsequently they had been withdrawn on the American demand. When Mikoyan came to Cuba, he confirmed to us that the agreement only provided for the withdrawal of the Soviet missiles. I asked him what would happen if the Americans demanded a withdrawal of the planes and the Soviet troops. He told me then: "To hell with Americans!"

However, in 24 hours the Soviet planes and the majority of the troops were withdrawn from Cuba. We asked why that had been done. The troops had been withdrawn without any compensation from the

American side! If the Soviet Union was willing to give us assistance in our defense, why did they agree to withdraw the troops, we were asking. At that time there were six regiments with 42,000 military personnel in Cuba. Khrushchev had withdrawn the troops from Cuba even though it was not required by the Soviet-American agreement. We disagreed with such a decision. In the end, as a concession to us the decision was made to keep one brigade in Cuba. The Americans knew about that brigade from the very beginning, but they did not discuss it. . . .

At the time of the crisis President Kennedy was under a great pressure, but he defended the official Soviet position. However, when he was shown the photos of the Soviet missiles in Cuba, he had to agree that the Soviets lied to him.

On the question of nuclear warheads in Cuba I can tell you that one day during the crisis I was invited to a meeting at the quarters of the Soviet Commander-in-Chief in Cuba at which all the commanders of different units reported on their readiness. Among them was the commander of the missile forces, who reported that the missiles had been in full combat readiness.

Soon after the Reagan administration came to power an American emissary, Vernon Walters, came to Cuba. We talked extensively about all aspects of our relations, and in particular, he raised the question of the October crisis. Trying to show how informed he was, he said that, according to his sources, nuclear warheads had not yet reached Cuba by the time of the crisis. I don't know why he said that, but according to the Soviet military, the nuclear missiles were ready for a fight.

I don't know what Khrushchev was striving for, but it seems to me that his assurances about the defense of Cuba being his main goal notwithstanding, Khrushchev was setting strategic goals for himself. I asked Soviet comrades about that many times, but nobody could give me an answer. Personally, I believe that along with his love for Cuba Khrushchev wanted to fix the strategic parity in the cheapest way. When the Soviet comrades proposed to us to deploy the nuclear missiles in Cuba I did not like the idea, but not because from the political point of view we would have been seen as a Soviet military base in Latin America. We were ready to accept the risk of an American military invasion of Cuba in order to avoid the political harm to the prestige of the Cuban revolution. But at the same time we understood that the Soviet Union needed that measure to ensure their own security. We knew that we had suffered a big political damage at the very time when we were dreaming about a revolution in all Latin America, but we were ready to make sacrifices for the Soviet Union.

SELECT BIBLIOGRAPHY

Allison, Graham, and Philip Zelikow. *Essence of Decision: Explaining the Cuban Missile Crisis*, 2nd ed. New York: Longman, 1999.

Ameringer, Charles D. *The Democratic Left in Exile: The Antidictatorial Struggle in the Caribbean, 1945–1959*. Coral Gables, FL: University of Miami Press, 1974.

Blight, James G., and Philip Brenner. *Sad and Luminous Days: Cuba's Struggle with the Superpowers after the Missile Crisis*. Lanham, MD: Rowman & Littlefield, 2002.

Brands, Hal. *Latin America's Cold War*. Cambridge, MA: Harvard University Press, 2010.

Castro, Fidel, and Ignacio Ramonet. *My Life: A Spoken Autobiography*. New York: Scribner, 2006.

Chang, Laurence, and Peter Kornbluh, eds. *The Cuban Missile Crisis: A National Security Archive Documents Reader*. New York: The New Press, 1992.

De la Cova, Antonio Rafael. *The Moncada Attack: Birth of the Cuban Revolution*. Columbus: University of South Carolina Press, 2007.

Dobbs, Michael. *One Minute to Midnight: Kennedy, Khrushchev, and Castro on the Brink of Nuclear War*. New York: Alfred A. Knopf, 2008.

Domínguez, Jorge I. *To Make a World Safe for Revolution: Cuba's Foreign Policy*. Cambridge, MA: Harvard University Press, 1989.

Friedman, Jeremy. *Shadow Cold War: The Sino-Soviet Competition for the Third World*. Chapel Hill: University of North Carolina Press, 2015.

Fursenko, Aleksandr, and Timothy Naftali. *Khrushchev's Cold War: The Inside Story of an American Adversary*. New York: W. W. Norton, 2006.

———. *One Hell of a Gamble: The Secret History of the Cuban Missile Crisis*. New York: W. W. Norton, 1997.

Gaddis, John Lewis. *We Now Know: Rethinking Cold War History*. New York: Oxford University Press, 1997.

Gleijeses, Piero. *Visions of Freedom: Havana, Washington, Pretoria, and the Struggle for Southern Africa, 1976–1991*. Chapel Hill: University of North Carolina Press, 2016.

———. *Conflicting Missions: Havana, Washington, and Africa, 1959–1976.* Chapel Hill: University of North Carolina Press, 2003.

———. *Shattered Hope: The Guatemalan Revolution and the United States, 1944–1954.* Princeton, NJ: Princeton University Press, 1991.

Holloway, David. *Stalin and the Bomb: The Soviet Union and Atomic Energy, 1939–1956.* New Haven, CT: Yale University Press, 1994.

Leffler, Melvyn P. *For the Soul of Mankind: The United States, the Soviet Union, and the Cold War.* New York: Macmillan, 2007.

LeoGrande, William M., and Peter Kornbluh. *Back Channel to Cuba: The Hidden History of Negotiations between Washington and Havana.* Chapel Hill: University of North Carolina Press, 2015.

Mikoyan, Sergo. *The Soviet Cuban Missile Crisis: Castro, Mikoyan, Kennedy, Khrushchev, and the Missiles of November.* Washington, DC, and Stanford, CA: Woodrow Wilson Center Press and Stanford University Press, 2012.

Paterson, Thomas G. *Contesting Castro: The United States and the Triumph of the Cuban Revolution.* New York: Oxford University Press, 1994.

Pavlov, Yuri. *Soviet-Cuban Alliance, 1959–1991.* Coral Gables, FL: University of Miami North South Center, 1996.

Pérez, Louis A., Jr. *The War of 1898: The United States and Cuba in History and Historiography.* Chapel Hill: University of North Carolina Press, 1998.

Rabe, Stephen G. *The Most Dangerous Area in the World: John F. Kennedy Confronts Communist Revolution in Latin America.* Chapel Hill: University of North Carolina Press, 1999.

———. *Eisenhower and Latin America: The Foreign Policy of Anticommunism.* Chapel Hill: University of North Carolina Press, 1988.

Rasenberger, Jim. *The Brilliant Disaster: JFK, Castro, and America's Doomed Invasion of Cuba's Bay of Pigs.* New York: Scribner, 2012.

Schoultz, Lars. *That Infernal Little Cuban Republic: The United States and the Cuban Revolution.* Chapel Hill: University of North Carolina Press, 2009.

Westad, Odd Arne. *The Global Cold War: Third World Interventions and the Making of Our Times.* New York: Cambridge University Press, 2005.

Zubok, Vladislav M. *A Failed Empire: The Soviet Union in the Cold War from Stalin to Gorbachev.* Chapel Hill: University of North Carolina Press, 2007.

Zubok, Vladislav, and Constantine Pleshakov. *Inside the Kremlin's Cold War: From Stalin to Khrushchev.* Cambridge, MA: Harvard University Press, 1996.